THE LAWS
OF
COURAGE

UNLEASH YOUR TRUE POTENTIAL
TO OPEN A PATH FOR THE FUTURE

RYUHO OKAWA

© 2009 by Ryuho Okawa
English translation © Happy Science 2009
Original title: "Yuuki-no-Hou"

Published by IRH Press Co., Ltd.
1-6-7 Togoshi, Shinagawa-ku,
Tokyo, 142-0041, Japan
Tel:81-3-6384-3771
Fax:81-3-6384-3778

First edition
Printed in Japan

ISBN-13: 978-4-87688-381-3
ISBN-10:   4-87688-381-3

Contents

Chapter Ⅲ Never Lose Your "Hungry" Spirit
Become a Different Person through Continuous Studying

Preface

We need more people who have courage in this world.

Our educational system continues to produce many adults who are afraid of making mistakes. It has a long way to go before it can receive a passing grade.

Do not fear failure. Failures are like trophies of your youth. You must gain something valuable out of them. As long as your aspirations are real, your life should be as passionate as a roaring fire.

Keep a "hungry" spirit within yourself and always continue to challenge new things. As long as you have the ambition to seek something higher, you will continue to grow.

Do not fear death. Rather, fear living a life where you do not accomplish anything. Stop making excuses, and push yourself to take a step forward.

Complete Virtue is acquired only when you gain wisdom, benevolence, and courage.

Ryuho Okawa
Happy Science
December 2008

Chapter I

Friendship and Courage

Doors Open to Those
Who Have Courage

THE LAWS OF COURAGE

Chapter I

Friendship and Courage

1. Attitude Changes Relationships

Friendships That Last and Those That Don't

I will begin this book with the topic of friendship and courage. While this theme is mainly for students and young adults, these words will help all readers to understand the attitude that is important to have in life.

I have always taught young people that getting an education is important, and that while young, they should invest in their futures by learning as much as they can. However, I feel that I have not taught enough about how the youth should develop relationships with other people.

So then, how should you form relationships when

you are young? The message that I have for the youth is that *friendships are more likely to succeed between two independent people.*

Some of you may think that friendship is a clingy relationship, but actually, this is not the case. There are some good aspects in this kind of extremely close friendship, but it is very likely that you will end up fighting with the other person. The friendship may even break off.

To build a good friendship that will last a long time, a certain degree of independence is needed from each person. If you are able to live sufficiently on your own, it is easier to form friendships. This goes the same for the people who you want as friends. Good relationships can form when each person is able to take care of themselves. These friendships are more likely to last longer.

However, friendships will easily crumble when one person must completely support the other, or when two people become desperately attached to each other because of selfish motives.

Finding Appropriate Distances
in Relationships

Many relationships fall apart because of the inability to keep an appropriate distance. For example, some people will come barging through the door of your comfort zone, and closely attach themselves to you at the slightest gesture of friendliness or the drop of a kind word. There are times that you do this to others, and times when others do it to you. These people barge in through your front door and settle themselves inside your house as soon as you open your door a crack with a small notion of interest or understanding. Friendships with these types of people are very hard to keep.

There are some people who think that true friendship is a relationship in which people are extremely attached together, but actually, it is rather difficult to form friendships with people who think in this way. Friendship is something that is built slowly, through a long span of time, while maintaining an appropriate amount of distance between the two. It may be better for you to build friendships little by little.

There is some danger in becoming "best friends" all

of a sudden, with very little time spent together. This is because in most cases, you do not know enough about the other person, and the other person does not know enough about you. It is important to build relationships slowly and without haste. You need to spend enough time getting to know each other. Use this method of taking things slowly and spending time to deepen your relationships.

If you are constantly forming and breaking friendships, not only will you be hurt but the other person will be hurt as well. The most common reason for hurting each other is a simple misunderstanding. You may misunderstand the other person, or the person may misunderstand you. As a result, you find yourself trapped in a difficult situation with that person and end up in a tragic separation. To build a relationship, a certain amount of distance between the two people is necessary. It is rare to share an instantaneous understanding with another person, so it is better to take relationships one step at a time.

In this way, at the level of casual friendship, you will be able to have a wide variety of relationships. With the casual relationships that will not progress further, there is no need to force a deeper relationship. If you do not push things too far and keep these relationships at a casual level, these friendships will be able to last for a long time.

2. Relationships Where No One Gets Hurt

How Much of Yourself Do You Show?

Relationships will deepen as you build it one step at a time. As you deepen your friendship, you will begin to share your deeper thoughts and feelings to apprehend the level of each other's friendship.

You share your thoughts and feelings with each other as if you are playing with cards. You play these cards of your thoughts and feelings, and you take turns courageously revealing them one at a time. In doing this, you see what kind of a hand the other person is playing with, and see whether it is strong or not. Being impressed with the strength of the other person's hand at times, you take turns turning over your cards.

As your friendship deepens, you start to play stronger and stronger cards. Take time to think about how far you would like to reveal your cards, and whether to play your final card or not.

How Far to Take Relationships

It is very difficult to completely understand each other. That is why it is best to maintain some distance if it seems like the relationship will end up hurting each other. If your relationship is one in which you can understand each other, then it is important that you think carefully about how far you can take it. If you come to a point where you cannot go any further with that relationship, it is probably best to stop at that level of friendship. Maybe something down the line will spur that friendship to an even deeper level. Also keep in mind that it may be difficult to form a friendship if you play too strong of a card at the very start of it.

When I was young, I found it relatively easier to make friends with people who had an understanding of religious matters. Even if they did not have a religious understanding, it was easier for me to talk to educated people who often read books. However, it became difficult when the relationship approached the level of faith. Therefore, in many cases, I would limit the relationship to the level of discussing our philosophies or views on life. I also found it most easy to talk with those who were ten to fifteen years older than I was. In my extensive reading of books in numerous fields, I suppose I had the opportunity to take a long, deeper look at my inner-self and at the matters of the world from a young age.

Since I mostly thought about the philosophies of life, it was difficult for me to make friends with people my own age. Most twenty year olds do not think about life too deeply, so there was not much that I shared in common with people my own age.

It is a good thing to keep in mind that if you share the same values to a certain degree, you can form friendships with people who are ten to fifteen years older. If you find that you have nothing to talk about with people your own age, try spending time with people a little older.

Playing the Card of Faith

In your hand, there are cards that represent your beliefs, or other aspects that involve the deepest parts of your mind. If you believe in a religion, this card would be the card of faith, and knowing when to play this card is the most difficult trick in the game.

For example, let us say you have a classmate who has a similar level of education as you, or a colleague in the office that has a similar position as you. If you do not play the card of faith, it is possible to keep a decent relationship at the worldly level with that person. However, very often when it comes to playing that card of faith, it is as if a towering cliff suddenly appears right in front of you.

If a person of faith is talking with a person that he or she finds attractive, and finds out that person is an outright materialist, it can be very sad. Even if you really like someone and think you want to date and marry that person, if that person has conflicting values, your future relationship will most likely be difficult.

In the end, a person's faith is the inner sanctuary of

that person's whole life. Faith is, in the truest sense, the final and best indicator of what kind of person he or she really is. If you both play your cards of faith and your friendship still remains as strong as ever, than you have come nearly to the last step. When it comes to faith, each person is at his or her own level, be it shallow or deep. Therefore, you must be very careful when playing your card of faith. The card of faith can only be played after your friendship has reached the level where you are completely open with each other.

You may happen to have a relationship between parent and child or between husband and wife where you have deep Dharma Connections and it is possible to have deep discussions without hiding anything. However, at the level of friendships, there will only be a few people in your lifetime that you will be able to truly call "Dharma Friends," or "friends on the path of Truth."

When it comes to faith, if you decide to take an all or nothing approach in your relationships with others, you will find yourself disappointed quite often. Both you and your friends will end up feeling hurt frequently. People may feel hurt or may end up hurting each other because of their clumsiness in relationships.

Therefore, it is important to play your cards little by little, and deepen your friendship as you carefully observe and evaluate how far you can take that relationship. This is a good way to build relationships with friends.

3. Do Not Be Carried Away by Bad Relationships

Choosing Mentor and Friends

In your days as a student or youth, an important choice that you have to make is whom you choose as your mentor and friends. The relationships between you and your mentor and friends will affect you greatly. These people will crucially influence your views on life and your future.

There are many difficulties in choosing your mentor and friends. A mentor is like the North Star who guides you to the path that you are going to take for the next several decades. That is why choosing a mentor is a difficult task. The same goes for choosing friends. If you choose the wrong friends, your path may bend one way or the other. Thus, it is important to think about whom you choose as your friends.

2,600 years ago, Shyakyamuni Buddha taught repeatedly not to make friends with foolish people and not to spend time with bad company. He taught that you would be better off walking alone, like a "rhinoceros' horn," than to be with those types of friends. He also taught to become friends with those that have greater qualities than you do, and with those who walk the path of the Truth. He often said, "If you cannot make good friends, then you should walk the path by yourself, as the lone horn of a rhinoceros."

In this way, Shakyamuni Buddha often used the metaphor of a rhinoceros horn in his teachings. The image of a one-horned rhinoceros walking alone does evoke a certain air of nobility. Through this, Shakyamuni Buddha was teaching that you should spend your time with those who are seekers of the Truth and those who have greater qualities than you. He taught that you would be better off alone than to mingle with bad people.

Just as there is a saying, "One rotten apple spoils the barrel," if you spend time with bad friends, you will find yourself slowly becoming like them. Unless you separate yourself from these types of people, you may find yourself an accomplice to their misdeeds because of your feelings of affiliation with them.

Friends Say What Needs to Be Said

We see a good deal of shoplifting among teenage students today. In many cases, it is not the act of an individual, but rather an act of a group. In addition to the person doing the actual stealing, there are sometimes lookouts, decoys or people pretending to be paying customers. It is easy for a group to pull off this thievery since convenience stores are usually only staffed by a single employee.

In this way, sometimes people form shoplifting gangs and steal together. These are examples of what you call bad friends, and when the group reaches numbers of five, six, seven or eight people, you will probably find it difficult to only sit out during the plans to shoplift.

If you try to sit out, the other members of the group would call you stuck-up and make threats to kick you out of the group. There may be times when you end up participating even though you do not wish to.

However, these kinds of friendships are evil. If anything, if you are really their friend, you have a responsibility to create a relationship where you can tell them that they should not do such things. The same goes for all of your friendships. There may be friendships that fall apart because you tried to stop them from doing something wrong. They may tell you that you are not good enough to be in the group, but you should not mind it even if that kind of friendship ends.

Just as Shakyamuni Buddha had taught, "Be as the horn of a rhinoceros and walk alone." Tell them, "If that is what it takes to be your friend, than I would rather go my way alone and live my life in pursuit of the Truth. Someday I will make friends who will follow the Truth with me, so I don't need you to be my friend."

As a friend, if you believe that your friends are doing

something wrong, you must have the courage to tell them that they are wrong. If you do not tell them, they may end up as criminals, or ruin the future that they could have had. That absolutely must not happen. You must say what needs to be said.

Bullying is a Miniature Copy of "Gang Activity"

Let us take for another example the social problem of bullying in schools. We can see a miniature copy of a "gang activity" in bullying today, as it is rare to see somebody bullied by a single person. In most cases, a "boss" leads his "thugs" to bully one person. Even though it is an unfair and dirty tactic, much of the bullying happens in the form of a large group ganging up on a small number of people.

However, many people in the group of bullies do not really want to bully others. They are just doing it out of fear of the leader. If they follow what the leader says, he or she will protect them and hang out with them. They constantly follow all the actions of the group because they fear exclusion from the group.

These groups of bullies, headed by their "bosses," pick on new students or transfer students who stick out. By participating in "bullying ceremonies" together, each person who is involved starts to feel like a member of the group. This feeling of belonging is similar to the criminal mentality that recognizes the fact that you took part in the bullying. It is the same as becoming a member of the gang if you take part in the robbery. Each member feels a sense of belonging with the others in the bully group, similar to that of a criminal gang, and participates in the bullying of others.

Therefore, even if they feel that bullying is wrong, they cannot just leave the group. By joining in on the bullying, they become accepted by the group and are protected from being bullied themselves. That is why the people who were once the target of bullying, eventually find themselves becoming a part of the group of bullies. The victim joins the group of bullies as soon as the focus of the bullying shifts to another person.

In this way, more and more people with the desire to be accepted join the group, multiplying their numbers and increasing their evil strengths. It is only one or two people at first, but it grows bigger and bigger to five, ten, or even twenty people. It comes down to the idea that there is nothing to be scared of if everybody does it.

An Evil Relationship is Like the Hierarchy in Hell

If there are ten or twenty students in a single class that are bullying one student, it is nearly impossible to pinpoint a single bully. Likewise, while the teacher would be able to scold a single student for bullying, when there are ten or twenty bullies against one victim, it is difficult for the teacher to punish all of those students just to protect one person.

For this reason, even if the teacher is aware of the bullying taking place, the teacher intentionally turns a blind eye. If the teacher came down on the group of bullies, which has become the predominant group in the class, chaos would break out, and the students would stop listening to the teacher. The students can decide to go on a strike against the teacher by refusing to listen to what the teacher says. In this situation, the teachers cannot punish the students. This is how evil continues to breed and grow.

This pattern is very similar to what happens in the realms of Hell in the spirit world. In Hell, just as the bullying at school, the strong demons induce the weaker demons and evil spirits to attack others. Since power is the basis of relationships in Hell, those who can slander the most people and can attack with the greatest strength are those who become leaders. A multitude of minions flock to those leaders and as a group, they bully those who are weaker than they are. On top of that, they are always looking for new recruits.

If you look at the bullying happening among the children, it is identical to what happens in the realms of Hell. The methods and approach of the children have a startling resemblance to the manners of Hell. From around elementary school, there are many children who are possessed by lower-level demons. There are even children who are possessed by demons that are much stronger. At the head of bullying groups of a certain size, there are leaders who have a relatively strong influence over other people. There may be times when powerful demons possess those leaders. You must not participate in these evil relationships. You must not be an accomplice to evil deeds.

4. Distinguishing Between Right and Wrong

Two Mentalities That Proliferate Evil

The spread of evil can be observed in many places of this world, but what is at the root of it all? One mentality that is at the root of evil is the democratic concept of majority rules, which was adopted post-World War II. This concept believes that the opinion of the majority is correct.

Taking again the example of bullying in schools, children think that the conduct of the majority of the class is correct. They think that since everybody is shoplifting, everybody is acting violently, and everybody is bullying together, it is the right thing to do, and that they will suffer a loss if they are not a part of that group. Therefore, one cause of evil is the idea that the majority determines what is correct.

Another cause is the traditional provincial mentality, which is especially prominent in the Japanese society. This idea states that everyone is the same. Therefore, if you are group conscious, and do exactly what everyone else is doing, you are correct. If you go against the conduct of the group, you are evil. In other words, this is a principle of ostracism, which judges that regardless of the situation, having a different opinion is wrong. To be different from the majority, to be apart from the group, or to act separately from the group is also undesirable. In reality, these mentalities exist as catalysts that spread evil.

Learn the Universal Rules of Right and Wrong

There are children who witness group criminal acts like bullying in schools, and immediately speak out against it. In many cases, they are usually children that have lived in a foreign country, or children who have parents that had spent time overseas. Additionally, there are children who have not been overseas, but have parents who attended missionary schools or other religious schools. If they were brought up with religious teachings, they tend to see the acts of group bullying as wrong.

However, the majority of people, who do not fall into these categories, tend to believe that the majority is right. Therefore, they often fall under the influence of the majority. The reason for this is that they do not have the basic understanding of what is right or what is wrong.

On the other hand, people who believe in, and act based on the morals taught by Buddha and God are not concerned with what the majority of a provincial society has to say. Such people do not think about saving themselves. Truth is the basis of their actions, and they do their best to determine what is right and what is wrong. Therefore, they can clearly say, "This kind of behavior is wrong," or "It is wrong to bully weaker people."

In my experiences, people who have spent time overseas are quite direct in saying something is wrong when they feel it is wrong. A lifestyle that transcends international borders requires certain standards or universal rules. That is why there are religious morals which surpass nationality or provincialism.

That is a reason why I strongly desire to change the Japanese education system so that children learn the religious concepts of right and wrong, and learn to have a global perspective.

Live with Greater Courage

To make the world a better place, we cannot yield our decisions to the principle of majority rule. We must consider what standards are universally right and wrong and act on them. Particularly, I ask the youth to have more courage. Those who cannot find courage in their youth will not find courage when they grow older.

It is common for those who are courageous in their youth to gradually stop saying what they really want to say and become more conservative as they settle down to raise a family, or as they start to have bigger responsibilities within their company. However, there is no chance for a person who lacked courage in their youth to find courage later in life. Even those who had courage will generally stop acting courageously as they run into a wall or are criticized.

Yet, the world needs people who will stand against this trend and speak justice. The world will not get any better if everyone yields to the opinion of the majority.

In all times, religion has wished for the betterment of the world and has pursued values that will realize righteousness. Religion teaches universal values, and because it has continuously taught that the worldly value system is wrong, religion has always had a revolutionary characteristic that works to change the values of this world.

In most cases, if it came down to a majority vote, religion would lose to worldly opinion. However, if we give up just because the world is run by majority, and think that nothing can be done if the majority thinks in this way, religious Truth cannot be found on Earth. If we compromise to the values of this world, religion will disappear from the face of the Earth.

If you truly desire to make the world a better place, you must keep trying, even if you face opposition, persecution and ordeals. No matter what way you put it, it takes courage to do what is right. I ask you to please, *have courage.* Please live a life full of courage.

5. Taking on Challenges Will Open Doors

Become an Intriguing Person

I want to address the youth on another point on the topic of courage. I wish for everyone to *become intriguing.* Many students and youth who are religious, are very dedicated and earnest, however the older generation feels that they are not very interesting people.

All religions emphasize submission and obedience to Buddha and God, and it is perfectly fine to earnestly follow the teachings. However, when people find you uninteresting as a person, it is not about your diligence. It is rather about the small range of your interest or the limit in the topics you can discuss.

When I was young, I was anything but boring. For example, when I was in my twenties, I spent some time in New York. My American friends often found me frank and humorous. Many American people tend to value those who are able to state their opinions because it makes it easier to know what they are thinking. Since I was like this, people thought of me as a captivating person.

I plead to the youth and students to be intriguing. Be interested in all sorts of things, and if you have something to say, say it. This is very important. Be a courageous person, and always voice your opinions. Do not fear setbacks or failure, and always be on the lookout for the next challenge.

Youthful People Do Not Fear Failure

As long as you are challenging yourselves, there will always be failure. People with high goals will definitely experience failure. Yet, those who fear failure have already consigned themselves to old age. They have given up their youth. This is because as people grow older, they naturally become more conservative and cautious without much effort. Little by little, they become more careful, and they gradually stop trying new things.

Some company executives, for example, cease to

innovate as they age, and the company forces them to resign. Times continue to change, but they have lost the ability to try new things. At a certain age, the company executives are asked to step down because of their age, and are effectively being run out of their company.

Not only is it natural for young people to have the spirit to try new things, it is essential. Even if an older person cautions you against it, you must have enough power to insist that you really want to try it. If you do not have that kind of power, you cannot call yourself young. Young people must keep on challenging without fear of failure. Those who claim that they have "never failed," are really saying that they have "never tried."

It is the same in the professional world. People who do not work do not fail. Yet, those who are ambitious and work with positive determination should experience many failures.

No new businesses can be created unless people keep on challenging. Only about one in ten people who create a new business will actually succeed. However, even if you know that, you must set your goals high and continue to challenge, or the path will never open before you.

If you are a student, you can say the same about sports. Some people participate in sports teams with the goal of one day becoming at least a benchwarmer. Maybe about half of those people will succeed in that goal. However, as they become regular members and start aiming for states or national playoffs, it becomes more difficult to accomplish their goals. In fact, if your goal is to win a gold medal in the Olympics, it is 99.99% likely that you will fail in that goal.

No matter what world you are in, the higher your goal, the higher the chance of failure. However, if you fear failure from the very start and do not even try, you will never be able to accomplish anything.

I have myself experienced many failures. As long as I try to accomplish new things, there will always be times when I fail. As long as I keep challenging myself, there will be failure. However, I continue to try in order to open the future for humankind. The way will remain closed if I fear failure and do not take challenges.

If you lower your goals, you will not fail as much. If you do nothing, you will not fail at all. However, these types of people are not taking any challenges. Do you really think it is good for you to end your life without ever taking on any challenges?

The biggest failure in life is to have never failed. To have never failed is the biggest failure that you can make in your lifetime. You must remember this. Those who experience much failure are those who have challenged themselves many times. Please do not fear failure. Go forth with courage, and challenge yourself.

Recognition Comes Later

I have discussed sports and business as examples, but the issue of how high to set your goals applies to all situations. The higher you set your goals, the greater the chance of failure. However, if what you are aiming for is in the right direction, you have interest or curiosity in it, and if you have the desire to try, please head straight towards that direction and pursue that path. I especially hope that the youth will make it a

The biggest failure in life is
to have never failed.

goal to become the foundation to usher in the new age.

This new age is not something a single person can create. It can only happen when many people come forth with their ideals and continue to take challenges. Although there may be many who fall on the way and figuratively pave the way with their bodies, there must be people who overcome those that fall. As more and more of these people come forth, the dawning of the new age will arrive. You must not be afraid of becoming a failure. Young people should have the mindset of wanting to go as far as they can, even if they fall to the ground along the way.

For that matter, I would hope that, if you do fall, you would serve as a boon and example to those who inherit your ideals after five, ten and twenty years. I hope that you will encourage them to surpass you, to learn from your mistakes, and to gain wisdom from your experiences. You should encourage them to go a much greater distance on the path.

I was criticized a great deal since I was young. As I worked as a religious leader, I was subjected to much more severe criticisms than most can imagine. Yet I did not let that affect me. As I worked hard telling myself, "I will not be defeated!" more and more people started to join me. The number of people who believed me grew, and Happy Science was established. Now, decades later, the criticism of the world is changing towards thinking, "Perhaps it was not just a big lie."

You can see that recognition comes along much later. Therefore, do not be the type of cowardly person who will not act unless they are immediately going to gain recognition. If you believe that something is right or something is true, then you must have the spirit to challenge towards it.

With a focus on friendship and courage, this chapter has discussed how to build relationships, the values of right and wrong, and the spirit of trying new things, which is an important mental stance you should take in living your life. Please do not fear solitude. Have the courage to lead a life of strength. I hope that this chapter will serve as a guide for you.

Chapter II

The Power to Endure Major Setbacks

Finding a New Perspective of Suffering

THE LAWS OF COURAGE

The Power to Endure Major Setbacks

1. Transforming Major Setbacks into "Harvests of Life"

The Positive Meanings of Major Setbacks

In this chapter, as I have titled "The Power to Endure Major Setbacks," I will mainly talk about the mindset that you should have when you are confronted with failure, suffering, and misfortunes in life.

I believe that there are many people who are searching for this kind of teaching in society today. Of course, people are happy when they succeed or experience victories in life, but in reality, it is very hard to spend an entire life on a continuous winning streak. The better the person gets at solving problems in life, the harder the challenges they will face. People who continue to succeed will set their goals higher, and people who continue to win will look for stronger opponents to compete against. Every person will come up against a wall at some point in their progression.

The first thing that you need to realize when you think about setbacks is that setbacks are not evil in themselves. From the perspective of this world, setbacks are seen as bad things and successes are seen as good things at the surface level. Yet from the deep perspective of the Truth, this is not always the case.

A short time ago, the "study of failure" received a lot of attention. The purpose of this study was to analyze the cause of certain failures in order to prevent future repetition. Studying how other people fail may be helpful to you because there are many similar patterns of failure. Studying what does not work out well for others will allow you to avoid the same mistakes to some degree, and from time to time, this knowledge may help you to overcome your own mistakes more easily. You can also learn to start the next day with a fresh and positive attitude without overwhelming yourself with worries, even if you do fail.

Failures can be converted into wisdom. If you are not aware of this perspective, you will lose much of the meaning of life. To begin with, religion teaches that this world is only a temporary world and that the true world is the world beyond this one. Living in this world is similar to leaving your hometown and traveling to a different country for a certain amount of time. You will make various mistakes throughout your journey, but in actuality, your travel destination is not the real world.

Humans are essentially spiritual beings that dwell within the physical body. The purpose of being born in this world is to gain experience as a soul. Failures and setbacks are a part of this experience, and it will remain in you as wisdom.

I have taught this over and over again, and it is in fact the Truth. Everybody should aim for the most fruitful life. If you look at your life with the perspective of harvesting for life, I believe that there are many things that can be gained from your experiences of setbacks and failures.

*The better the person gets
at solving problems in life,
the harder the challenges they will face.*

Wisdom Within Setbacks

If you look from a broader point of view, setbacks are present at the level of the nation as well. Losing a war is an example of such setback.

Japan fought and won against China in the Sino-Japanese War and against Russia in the Russo-Japanese War. While participation was very limited, Japan was also on the winning side of World War I. At that time, Japan had grown arrogant because the country had won three times in a row. The people of Japan believed that if Japan went to war, the *kamikaze* ('sacred wind') would blow and grant victory to the divine land of Japan. This is why Japan was defeated in World War II in such a tragic way.

It is a hard and terrible experience to be defeated in war, and Japan's defeat in World War II was without a doubt, a nationwide setback. However, I feel that what Japan was able to learn from losing was very significant. Considering that Japan has prospered for more than 60 years following the end of World War II, I think we can say that the people of Japan were able to reflect on themselves because of their defeat, and were able to become very humble. Their prideful noses were broken, and they realized that it was wrong to become arrogant and haughty. The citizens of Japan, as a whole nation, were truly able to start all over again.

The diligence of the citizens brought forth fruits of labor and ushered in the post-war prosperity that we know today. At the end of the war, I am sure no one had any idea of the prosperity that awaited Japan. If we only look at the defeat, we only see the tragic ending, but to the people of Japan, the experience of defeat had spurred a breakthrough.

As you can see from this example, continuous victory can lead to arrogance, even on a national level. Japan had technically won three wars in a row beginning with the Sino-Japanese War, but in reality, the Russo-Japanese War was only won by judgment. Japan was only able to win that war because the United States had served as a mediator. In fact, Japan no longer had the strength to continue fighting, and it is actually a wonder that Japan even proved victorious. Even if it is a battle that you normally would not have won, if you just happened to win by chance, there are times when your way of thinking will start to slack.

Grasp Your Chance to Breakthrough in Life

The pattern of continuous success leading to arrogance and failure can also be seen at the level of the business world.

Konosuke Matsushita (1894-1989), the founder of Panasonic, said, "It is not too good to succeed continuously. It is better for you to fail once after succeeding three times." Of course, Matsushita was not encouraging us to fail. As people continue to succeed, they become conceited and careless. They become arrogant, lose sight of themselves, and end up committing big, destructive mistakes. However, one failure for about every three successes or so has a sobering effect on a person. It is like the salt added to a dish that brings all the flavors together. Failures help people to reflect on themselves, and instill in them the desire to become humble. Matsushita's words are those of an expert in life.

When people think that they simply keep on winning, there are times when they are actually just lacking an objective judgment of their situation. It is also possible that they are actually not fighting real battles, and that they are not challenging themselves at all.

If you think that failure and setbacks are nothing more than bad things and that avoiding them is the way to succeed in life, you are mistaken. By doing this, you may be missing a big chance to breakthrough or a great opportunity for your spirit to transform and blossom. This is a characteristic of failures and setbacks that you must realize.

2. Perspectives and Attitudes Resilient to Setbacks

Looking from a Different Angle

The wealthier the society gets, the greater our wants become. The greater our wants become, the higher the hurdle for satisfaction becomes. People compare themselves with others, and they suffer from a matter of winning or losing. However, there is more than one way to look at things. By changing the way you look at a certain situation, you may find something other than suffering in failure and setbacks. Here are some specific examples of how this is true.

Transforming Your Perspective 1:

A Change in Setting Can Change Your View
Compared to India, Tokyo Looks Like a Futuristic City

First, let us take the perspective of your setting. Some of you who are reading this book may feel unsatisfied with the situation you are in. Perhaps you are suffering because of that. However, to someone from another country, the place where you live may appear quite different from how you see it. A while ago, right when I returned to Japan after spending two weeks in India, it felt as if I had come to a city from the future. As I was returning to Tokyo from Narita Airport, I was surprised at how smooth the roads in Japan were. It almost felt as though I was in a flying saucer gliding through space. That is how smooth the drive was.

Before going to India, I had never thought of Japan's roads beyond that of having a lot of traffic, or that there are a lot of cars. I was never aware that we were in fact, driving on a smooth road. However, when I was visiting Buddhist historic landmarks in the countryside of India, we drove on roads that were hardly paved and were littered with potholes. After we drove on roads bumpy enough to knock the tires off our car, I realized just how perfectly paved the roads in Japan were. As you can see, things can appear different when you look at them from a different angle.

Transforming Your Perspective 2:

Your Life is Not Your Educational Background
The More Prestigious the School, the Higher the Suicide Rate

When I think about what the youth are suffering from, I think about the hurdle of being accepted into a good school. I can imagine how difficult it must be to be at the stage of "exam wars" in your lives. Yet, compared to the countries where people do not have sufficient opportunity to receive an education, it could be said that you are blessed to live in a country where you have many chances to learn. It is my hope that you will have this perspective too.

Also, since schools today are usually ranked based on percentile, whether an applicant scores high or low on their exams can mean success or failure for the applicant. However, getting into a good school does not necessarily guarantee success, nor does getting into a lower-level school guarantee failure. For example, there are people who point out that the suicide rate is higher in schools that are harder to get into.

Happy Science has been involved in the Fight Against Suicide Campaign for a few years now, but it is not necessarily the case that people who have hit rock bottom of their lives will commit suicide or that successful people will not commit suicide. There are actually many people who commit suicide because they experience a major setback after achieving some level of success.

Though this is an episode that happened more than thirty years ago, when I had just enrolled into Tokyo University, I heard something that still has an impression on me today.

One day a certain professor addressed us in a large lecture hall. He said, "Every year, at least one LAC I student commits suicide, however, LAC II students do not commit suicide" (LAC is an acronym for "Liberal Arts Core"). Students in LAC I are generally those who aspire to become government officials or legal professionals. LAC II includes students who are enrolled in the Faculty of Economics, and consists mainly of students who find jobs in business corporations after graduating.

The professor told us, "LAC I is full of people who were academically at the top of their high schools back in their hometowns. So these people, who cannot stand being anything but the best, cannot handle the setbacks and resolve to committing suicide. Be careful because this kind of perspective and way of thinking is not correct."

Of course, there will always be a ranking from the highest to the lowest, even if all the students were at the top of their high schools back in their hometowns. However, there are some students who cannot accept this.

People who already have a little sense of giving up are stronger against setbacks. Those who cannot handle being acknowledged as anything but the very best can easily turn to suicide. People who were successful in the beginning may suffer when their paths start to close up along the way. Some people think it is unacceptable that their life is not opening up for them constantly so they impulsively commit suicide when something goes wrong.

On the other hand, students who go to schools that are not as prestigious tend to know their place at an earlier stage and do not set expectations that are out of their reach. People who do not consider themselves to be "the best in the world" will not turn to suicide so easily. When the lives of those types of people start blooming, everybody is surprised. Even if they had entered a school that is not prestigious, there are people whose lives start going well at a certain stage in life.

Transforming Your Perspective 3:

Building Immunity to Setbacks

Failure Early in Life Builds Immunity Against Future Setbacks

Though this may be an extreme example, there are homeless people who live competing with the birds for food that others threw away and even find shelter in the streets. Still, they are living quite robustly.

On the other hand, there are CEOs and department heads of large companies who commit suicide when their companies are on the verge of bankruptcy. Compared to homeless people, these executives have social positions that are as different as Heaven and Hell. Yet people who are in the more favorable positions are actually choosing to end their life. There are also people who graduate with excellent grades from Tokyo University's Faculty of Law and get a job with the Ministry of Finance, only to commit suicide, lamenting life because they had lost in the race of promotion.

When you think about who the real winner or loser in life is, you probably would not choose someone praised for their brilliance in the beginning, but ended up jumping off a building to die. I must say that this kind of life is rather miserable.

Even if it does not result in suicide, there are always failures at work. Each person has within them the ability to endure those failures. How much failures and adversities you can endure is actually a measure of your capability in life.

Setbacks come swiftly to those who always feel the need to be praised and admired like delicate flowers by everyone around them. However, there are also people who have struggled to live. They live their lives like a flounder or halibut crawling on the ocean floor, constantly changing colors to blend in with the sand. Sometimes these people have a much broader view of the world and can understand the average standards and the norms of this world better. There are cases where these types of people gradually become tougher, and live without losing to adversities.

People who experience a lack of recognition, unhappiness, or frustration earlier in life gain a certain immunity which makes them stronger. In that light, while I understand that students are having a rough time with passing exams, a part of me wants to tell them, "Challenge yourself to the fullest, but don't worry even if you fail."

Those who experience failure early in life will build immunity to future failure. The lesson to learn is that the world is not that easy. This is a very valuable thing to know. Realizing that the world does not march to your own personal drum will have a sobering effect on your perspective on things. Also, failure can leave you with a toughness that allows you to see other paths when one does not go the way you wanted it to.

There are many people who think they must fulfill certain requirements in order to find happiness, but I believe that there is a problem with this way of thinking.

Transforming Your Perspective 4:

There is More to People than What Meets the Eye

The Secret Burden of Being Beautiful

If you are a woman, you may think that women who are born beautiful are happy. However, I think it would be pretty difficult if you actually were to live a life as a beautiful woman.

Recently, we hear a lot about stalkers, but the problem of women being chased around by men has always existed. Men would wait for them on their way to school or work and bombard them with letters and phone calls. The beautiful have to go through many of these bothersome experiences.

It would be great if they had one wonderful man who loved them very much, but it must be very hard to be liked by too many people. When you receive "vibes" from other people, even if you are not psychic, you feel as if there are many ghosts clinging onto you. It is not a very pleasant experience. Since my spiritual eyes are open, I know exactly how these "vibes" feel like. I am sure that being beautiful can be hard work.

Transforming Your Perspective 5:

There Are Two Sides To a Coin

People Who Are Slaves to Money.
People Who Become Diligent After Debt.

Next, I will discuss the issue of money. Money can be for the good or for the bad. Most old religions teach that money is evil and that it will lead to your ruin.

In reality, people actually do stop working hard once they develop some leeway in their wallets. The average person will not roll up his or her sleeves and concentrate on work unless there is a pressure of having to repay a loan or having some other responsibility.

Eight out of ten people would probably fall into this category.

People have many different motivations for working. For example, some people may have a 30 year mortgage to buy a house, so they cannot quit their job until retirement. They might have to pay for their child's education, or perhaps their business went under so they have to work hard to make up the difference. Though it is a sad fact, there are more people in the world who will work if they owe someone money, but will not work without that motivation.

On the other hand, when people have a little extra money, they easily let their guards down. There are probably many people like the main character in Ryunosuke Akutagawa's (1892-1927) novel, *Toshishun*, who immediately treats many people to go out drinking and singing, and splurges as soon as they obtain a large amount of money.

The same principle applies to studying as well. Average students tend to slack off when they see a bigger raise in their grades compared to the efforts they made. They will only start trying harder when their grades start to drop.

The same holds true for marriage. To a young man, a certain woman may look beautiful and he may want to marry her. Yet in reality, after getting married, he will have to work for decades to support his family. In other words, he is putting up his future as a sort of collateral at an early stage in his life. Marriage is like taking out a huge loan. In order to raise his family, he has to work hard for the next several decades to repay the "debt."

In one sense, marriage and other structures of this world are put together quite well. Though it leans towards the view that human nature is fundamentally flawed, I feel that such systems take well into account the laxity, conceit, and arrogance of humankind.

Transforming Your Perspective 6:

People Make Effort Because They Want Something More

The Ingenious Mechanisms of Life That Make Up for the Laxity of People

It is often the case that people work hard when they feel they are lacking something. Yet, when that motivation is gone, people immediately start to slack off and become lazy. Since human beings do have these characteristics, if a social structure was created to make a perfectly equal society, people would cease to work, and it would lead to the deterioration of society.

For example, in the world of professional baseball or soccer, there is a huge gap in pay between the star players who make millions of dollars and the average players who do not. If all players made the same amount of money, regardless of their abilities or achievements, do you think that they would earnestly try their best? In this sense, differences in remuneration have an aspect that leads to each player's seriousness, which makes the game more interesting.

Looking at the big picture, the various gaps that exist between people bring diversity to our world and create the potential for each person to make efforts in their own path. This is a concept that is important to understand.

Transforming Your Perspective 7:

Look At Yourself Objectively
Is Your Dream Influenced by the Values of Others?

The next topic I would like to talk about is to take another look at yourself from an objective point of view.

I believe that if everybody looked back on their lives from the time they were a child until they became an adult, almost everybody would be surprised at the number of things that they have failed to accomplish.

At different points in life, you may have felt that you wanted to become a certain way, but you may realize that most of those wishes never came to pass. However, after a certain age, your feelings towards the times you were not able to realize yourself will start to change. You will begin to think, "It was all for the best. After all, I was able to discover a path of my own because of that."

A great majority of the dreams of young people never come to fruition. Among those wishes, there are some that come straight out of that person's own feelings. However much of the desires of young people are influenced by the values of others. Their desires are influenced by what their friends are saying, what all their friends want to do, or what their parents wish for them.

There are many crossroads in life, but we can only choose one path. It is impossible to walk more than one path at the same time. Even if you wish to choose the path that everyone else wants to follow, there are cases when this path will be blocked off, and stop you from going forward. In these times, you will feel very sad.

However, your path will gradually start to reveal itself, and you will realize the importance of walking your own path. You will come to understand that you have to walk your own path and that you will not be satisfied with any other. One day, you will feel glad that you did not choose to live the life of somebody else.

You are a being that continues to be reincarnated from the other world to this world many times. The reason you are born on Earth in this lifetime is to obtain a new unique personality from all of your experiences in life. Since you were born to gain new personal qualities in this lifetime, you do not have to be the same as everyone else. Enjoy your differences with other people. Find delight in your uniqueness.

Going where everyone else wants to go is in one

sense, the same as setting yourself up for a life full of suffering. The place where everyone else wants to go is most likely not the path of happiness for you. That is why you need to be able to look at yourself with an objective eye.

Transforming Your Perspective 8:

"Happiness to Me is..."
The Path Envied by Everybody is Not Necessarily Better

In this world, there are a few elites that have jobs that everyone is jealous of. However, it does not mean that these people are free from worries. Although they may appear to be walking a path that is far from setbacks, if you were to peer into their minds, you would find that they are suffering from their own sense of failure.

Setbacks on the Path to Becoming a Doctor

Let us examine the life of a person whose goal is to become a doctor and see what can be learned about the life of the elite.

Let us assume that there are those who wanted to become a doctor ever since they were in elementary school or junior high school. In order to become a doctor they must go to medical school. However, most universities only accept about 100 students into their medical schools, so it is very difficult to get in. Thus, there are many people who fail at the stage of the entrance exams to get into medical schools. The inability to get into medical school is the first setback they may experience.

Even if they are accepted into medical school, they still have to pass the National Examination in order to become a licensed doctor. Not everybody passes this exam, so unfortunately, there will always be people who fail. Every year, only 80-90% of those who take the National Examination for Medical Practitioners will pass. Some of these people take the exam again and again but still do not pass. So there are people who cannot become doctors even if they attended medical school.

It must be disappointing for people to fail their entrance exams, but it is just as disappointing to pass the entrance exam, only to fail in actually becoming a doctor. This is another setback they may experience.

After graduating medical school and start working as a resident, there are people who realize that being a doctor is not right for them. Though it is very unfortunate, there are people who realize that they entered medical school because they had good grades, but being a doctor does not actually suit them. What is more necessary in becoming a doctor is actually the study of human relationships rather than the classes in physics, math or English. Doctors have to work with people all day. So it would be quite tragic if someone who liked to study but did not like people became a doctor.

There are many people who perform well on the test subjects in medical school, but because they do not like people, they experience setbacks once they actually become doctors.

Setbacks in Life After Becoming a Doctor

There are some people who become doctors and want to stay and work at the university hospital. However, not everybody will be given the opportunity to stay.

There are also doctors who open their own practices. While there are private practice doctors that gain a high income and succeed, there are also others who become saddled with debt they cannot repay and suffer. When doctors cannot repay their debt and suffer in deficit, some of them will tell their patients that they are very sick when they are not, and though they feel guilty, they prescribe unnecessary medicine and hospitalize patients longer than needed. They know they should not, but there will be people who do things that prick at their consciousness.

Even those who remained in the university hospital go through many trials. It may appear that those who earned their desired positions at the university hospitals are happy and those who had to leave are unhappy. However, there are many paths that branch out even for the people who stayed at the university hospitals.

The hierarchy at university hospitals is extremely strict and feudalistic. Some people cannot handle this kind of environment. In the first place, people that are exceptional at their studies tend to struggle with interpersonal relationships. So there are actually many people who have trouble getting along with others in the university hospitals. These types of people are literally suffering to the point of suffocation under the feudalistic and closed-off system.

There is also preferential treatment when it comes time for transfers. Those doctors who did not butter up to the professor to gain favor may find themselves relegated to a less desirable position.

Unfortunately at university hospitals, there are also cases when doctors are demoted because they told the truth. There are people who tell the truth about malpractice even though an order had been given to keep quiet. The doctor's conscience prods him to tell the family of the deceased that the patient should have survived, and that the patient only died because of a mistake that the doctor made. Through this, the malpractice is discovered and the police come to investigate the hospital. The honest doctor is seen as "the person who leaked the information," and ends up being demoted. Even if the action was righteous, it may result in a temporary setback in this world.

What is more, even if some doctors rise to the position of a renowned professor at a national university, they may be ruined when other people find out they were taking bribes from pharmaceutical companies. These sorts of things happen because even if they were excellent as doctors, they did not know enough about the law. These kinds of professors accept monetary gifts because they do not know where the line is drawn for what is considered a bribe and what is not.

Other than this, there are some doctors who embezzle university funds, get caught, and fall from their position. As you can see, even doctors, who are generally considered elite, are prone to various setbacks. Many of them will continue to drop out one after another.

Setbacks Come to Even the Best Doctors

There are also people who experience regret after they had made a name for themselves as great doctors and gained the title of a professor.

There is a famous anatomist who was made an emeritus professor at a university hospital for his lectures on the topic, "All things originate from the brain." He taught that the human mind was simply a brain function and that the brain is all and everything.

One of his students fell into a mislead religion and

committed a terrible crime. This could be considered a setback on the part of the professor.

I am sure that the professor suffered, wondering why his former student would join such a cult. This particular student had a spiritual experience in the cult he joined. He was shocked to realize that the spiritual world really did exist and began to think that the theory his professor had taught him in college was all a lie. Later on in his life, he became a devoted follower and played a big role in promoting this cult which made lethal gas.

However, within spiritual phenomena, there are good types and bad types. Many of these phenomena are actually caused by evil spirits. To this day, that professor still has not realized that it was because of his mistaken theory that his student joined that cult. He may think that it is only natural that doctors reject mystical powers, faith and religion, but this is a very naïve attitude. There are people who believe in mystical powers and the power of faith, even if they are well known doctors.

Take for example, Alexis Carrel (1873-1944), a

Nobel Laureate in Physiology or Medicine. When Carrel visited the Fountain of Lourdes (France), which is known for its miraculous healing properties, he witnessed miracles of people being healed of their incurable diseases and accredited the healing to some mystical power (see *The Voyage to Lourdes*, *Man, the Unknown*, and *Reflections on Life*, all authored by Carrel). So you can see that medicine and religion are not completely incompatible. It just means that the doctors who reject religion have lived in a world that is lacking spiritual knowledge and experience.

In this manner, even if people had climbed to the top of the social ladder as doctors and appear successful, there are times when setbacks will come to them later in life.

Some Setbacks Turn Out to Be for the Better
Defeat in the Anpo Toso Gave Birth to the Prosperity of Japan

Above, I shared with you various examples of how there is more than one way to look at things. In the same way, if you look back on past setbacks after a certain period of time, there are times when you realize that the setback was actually for the better. As an example of this, I would like to talk about the *Anpo Toso* (the opposition movement to the Treaty of Mutual Cooperation and Security between the United States and Japan.)

I was a university student during the times shortly following the *Anpo Toso* riots of the 1970s. There was an air of disappointment among students on campus at that time, and a great deal of mistrust between professors and students still lingered. There are quite a few people among the Baby Boomer generation who participated in this opposition when they were university students and experienced a sense of failure. The defeat of the opposition movement may have been an experience of dismay for everyone who participated in the student demonstrations.

Anpo Toso refers to the opposition movement against the Treaty of Mutual Cooperation and Security (*Anpo Jyoyaku*) between the United States and Japan. There were two major movements in *Anpo Toso*; one in the 1960s and another in the 1970s.

During that time, many students barely studied and they spent all their time in the opposition movement.

Though the movement had failed in the end, it can be said that Japan was able to prosper because of this failure. The Security Treaty still remains in force today and because of it, Japan and the United States are able to keep a military alliance.

The Prime Minister Who Kept to His Beliefs

The largest skirmish was in the 1960s *Anpo Toso* when Prime Minister Kishi was in office. During that time, the residence of the prime minister was also surrounded by demonstrators. I have read materials with inside information that documented this incident. The materials stated that the security force told the prime minister, "Please escape. We cannot protect you any longer. The police do not have enough power. This is a revolution, and we cannot guarantee your life." Even in this dangerous situation, Prime Minister Kishi firmly believed that the Security Treaty would benefit Japan, and struck out to amend the treaty.

Kishi announced his resignation soon after this incident, but he was later stabbed by a thug in the thigh and was wounded badly. This truly was an age on the verge of a revolution. However, looking back at the results of that age, I believe that the decision to preserve the Security Treaty was correct, even though there were more people against it at that time.

What Saved Japan

If the government had given into the left wing, disaffirmed the Security Treaty and joined forces with the former Soviet Union and China, Japan surely would not have enjoyed the prosperity that followed. If the Security Treaty was disaffirmed, a terrible, tragic period may have awaited Japan. Tens of millions of citizens may have been slaughtered. There was even the fear of many people being arrested and killed for committing an ideological offense.

At that time, North Korea was called a "paradise on Earth" and everyone thought it was an ideal nation. Many Japanese citizens participated in the *Anpo Toso* in their desire to make Japan a country like North Korea, but in reality, those people had been manipulated with incorrect information and were seeing a delusion of North Korea.

If Japan had taken the path to become a country like North Korea, a great misfortune would have come over the country. Situations in Japan would have been like Hell. If Japan had become like North Korea, many people would have been put to death. However, all of this was avoided because the government chose to maintain the treaty. As you can see, many people experienced setbacks during the *Anpo Toso*. Yet when you look at the results, the defeat suffered had turned out to be a good thing.

A Political Scientist Who Evaded "The Worst"

In the 1960's, one of the main pillars of the ideology behind Anpo Toso was Masao Maruyama (1914-1996). Maruyama was a professor of political science at Tokyo University at that time, and he fueled the opposition movement using his position as a scholar. However, as I stated before, the opposition failed. With that huge setback, Maruyama soon quit his job as a professor and did not accomplish anything of significance for the rest of his life.

When I spiritually checked to see where he went after he died, I found out that he went not to Heaven, but to Hell. Maruyama was not bad as a person. He was somewhat a genius as a scholar and was well respected. The study of political science at Tokyo University was even called "Maruyama-esque," and he had many students.

Why did a man so revered go to Hell? It was because he led people on a path of misguided ideologies. Maruyama experienced a major setback through this movement and resigned his position as a professor because of it. Yet, it can be said that Maruyama's setback was a "correct setback" for him. It was actually better for him to have experienced this setback while he was still alive. If the opposition movement had been successful, he would have fallen even further into Hell, to be called Satan (the devil). He may have become a demon that confuses and mislead many people to the wrong path.

I remember watching the scene of the opposition movement on television. It was right before I entered Junior High School. I watched students wearing helmets and masks as they held themselves up in the Tokyo University Yasuda Lecture Hall. I also watched the troops surround the students and turn water hoses on them.

Those students boycotted their classes, caused entrance examinations to be cancelled and caused a lot of trouble for many people. In the end, it can be said that their actions were a type of regression phenomena. They were all returning to an infant mentality. I believe that the backbone of this movement was students who did not want to grow up. Without feeling any social responsibility as an adult, they just wanted to act violently.

When it comes to a large-scale movement such as a revolution, even if the wills of a large number of people are united, it may fail. Yet, if the goal of the movement is wrong to begin with, it may have been for the better that they had failed. There seems to be many people who participated in the *Anpo Toso* who still harbor feelings of disappointment, but I would like these people to be aware of this perspective as well.

3. How to Cope with Setbacks

There is yet another thing that I would like to share with everyone. Currently there are 120-130 million people living in Japan and more than six billion people in the world. Each person has their own idea of their path to success. However, because there are so many people living in this world, we experience competition in many aspects of life. It is only natural that someone else may take what you want, and that you may try to ruin one another. There will be things that do not turn out the way you wanted.

For example, if there is more than twice the number of applicants to a school than the number of students accepted, more people will be denied than accepted. This goes the same in job hunting and promotions. In many situations in society, the more people with the same goals, the harder it will be for one person to realize that goal.

Though you may wish to become a doctor or the president of a company, it is not that simple to actually become one. Even if you were employed by a prestigious company, most people will not become the president of that company. Even if you start your own business and get the title, there are times when the company goes under.

Things generally do not go the way we want them to in this world. Life is full of setbacks, and no matter who they are, those who seek to better themselves will experience them. However, while you cannot avoid a setback itself, how you accept it and deal with it will separate you from others. Each person handles setbacks in different ways.

Different Levels of Dealing with Setbacks

Level 1: Become Desperate

Some people become desperate and run amuck when they experience major setbacks. They may become violent at home or in public, and start holding grudges against the world because of a setback they experience. This is the lowest level of coping with setbacks.

Level 2: Endure Suffering

Some people, even if they are sad and in pain after failing, they will hang in there. They will suppress their sadness and endure the suffering and pain of failure. Those who fall into this group belong to the next level up of coping with setbacks.

Level 3: Unable to Handle Successive Setbacks

One small step up from those who endure suffering is those who somehow recover their calmness after a setback as they tell themselves, "Yes, I made a huge mistake, but I'll get another chance. I can keep going." However, should these people experience a chain of multiple setbacks, they break down and become reckless. These are the type of people who come in just below average on the coping scale.

People who do not go crazy after one setback, but become reckless after their second or third time and start holding grudges against other people or the world, rank a little below average in coping with setbacks.

Level 4: Strive to Overcome

There are also people who experience multiple setbacks and are in a state of sadness and pain, but will somehow endure it and persevere to take the best path they can. These people are at a little higher level than the average person.

Level 5: Find Providence in Setbacks

So what kind of people would rank in the top levels of coping with setbacks? These are the types of people who see themselves from the perspective of a higher world. These people can find providence (the Will of Heaven) in their setbacks. When they fail, they can consider to a certain degree about whether they have mistaken their course in life, or whether their destiny or path lies somewhere other than in the direction they are heading.

As 10, 20, and 30 years pass since you were born, you may think you know the right path to follow, as it is reinforced by the knowledge and experiences gained throughout life and by the opinions of others. In spite of this, things sometimes do not turn out the way you planned, and you experience failure as a result. In this case, it is important to know that there is a limit to both your own knowledge and experience as well as a limit to the advice that your parents and others around you can give. That is why you should try to perceive the greater providence at work.

Level 6: Find Seeds of Happiness in Setbacks

The level above this is people who not only feel the promptings of providence, but also make effort to find seeds of happiness in their setbacks. These people feel the Will of Heaven and accept their failures as karma or assignments from a previous life. They understand that the inability to pursue their original path as a part of their training in this life. However, they do not stop with simply accepting this as a fact. They go a step further and look for seeds of happiness in their setbacks. This is the highest level of coping with setbacks.

Change Setbacks into Success
Systematically Dispose Your Past Self to Make a "New You"

I mentioned above about finding seeds of happiness in setbacks. At the beginning of this chapter, I also discussed the study of failure. Through this, I wanted to point out that the seeds for your next success are found within what appears to be your failures.

If you are always successful, you may not know exactly why you have succeeded. However, a failure will awaken you to at least one realization. Through failure, you will be able to realize that whatever you have been doing will not work. By analyzing your failures, you will be able to yield seeds of future success.

It is unacceptable just to chalk your failures up to fate, or to blame the world for this and that. It is vital that you analyze and learn from your failures. There are no new successes on the path that you have already succeeded in. If you are to challenge yourself and seek new horizons, you must adapt to new surroundings and systematically let go of your former self. Unless you systematically let go of your former self and develop a

... the seeds for your next success are found within what appears to be your failures

"new you," you will never achieve anything more than what you already have.

When setbacks or failures fall onto you, you must find the seeds of happiness that will bring future success. You must find your new self. You must comprehend that it is because of your failure that you are actually able to transform into a "new you" and progress. You need to make the most of your failures and develop the qualities and abilities that are already within you.

A long time ago, there was a *Sumo* wrestler who said, "When you are thrown to the ground, unless you taste the dirt of the ring and engrave in your mind the imprint your body has left in the dirt, you will never become an *Ozeki* or *Yokozuna* (second highest and highest ranked sumo wrestlers)." What he was saying was that in order to change yourself, you need to have the discipline within you to learn from your defeats.

There are people who do not resign everything to good or bad fortune but endure their failure and thoroughly think through their mistakes. By contemplating on their failures, they identify the reason of their failure and are able to find seeds of success within it. These people have a different attitude to begin with. They are able to analyze the aftermath of their defeat and turn their thoughts to the future.

4. The Highest Road in Life

Live Your "Own Life" All the Way Through

I have had all kinds of experiences in my life. When I was young, I had no idea that I would become a religious leader, so I walked a number of paths much different from the path that I had originally planned. However, I believe that all of these experiences have helped me in many different ways. It is better to believe that it is sometimes good that we do not know what lies ahead in life.

It is vital that you work with all your strength to progress, but you should also grasp providence in the successes and failures that appear in front of you. You must calmly decipher where the Will of Heaven is directing you.

If you have a mind that wishes only for your own

good, you will not be able to understand everything. With a self-centered perception, there are things you just cannot understand. You need to humbly learn and comprehend what Heaven is trying to teach you through your successes and failures.

Lastly, tell yourself this: "The greatest life for me is the life that brings the best out of me. I will not become happy by living a life of somebody else. The best life for me is one where I can grow to my fullest potential through a position, job and lifestyle that I am best suited for. It is best for me to live in accordance with the Will of Heaven and walk a path where my own talents and progressions are developed to the fullest."

You must not allow yourself to be swayed by the values and standards of others. There are times in life when you must listen to what others are saying, but there are also times when you must not listen to them, no matter how much they tell you to. It is important that you live out your life according to your own principles.

Dealing with Misfortune
The Life of an Apple Orchard Owner

There is a story that I read when I was a student that remains with me to this day, and it is about how to cope with misfortune. It is a story introduced in a book called *Hiun ni Sho Suru Michi* ('The path to cope with misfortune'), and it is written by Kojin Shimomura (1884-1955), the author of *Jiro Monogatari*.

In this book, there is a dialogue between Shimomura and a young apple farmer who became very successful in his twenties. Shimomura asked the young apple farmer what the hardest thing he had experienced since he started the apple orchard. The young apple farmer talked about the typhoon that hit the orchard in his first year of work. He said that he was about to go insane when he saw the apples that he had spent so much time growing being slammed into the ground. However, the young apple farmer said that through changing his attitude, he no longer suffered from the damages made by the typhoons. His words are as follows.

"Typhoons are a natural phenomenon, and since they come every year, you have to be prepared for them. Apples are blown off because they are not in accords with providence. Apples that are deemed fit by the Will of Heaven will definitely stay on the branch. No matter how fierce the typhoon is, aren't there always apples that remain on the tree? This is the attitude I chose to embrace." This attitude is important. The farmer could not stop the typhoons from coming in order to protect his apples. For him, it may have been the turning point of his life when he decided to grow apples that can endure typhoons.

Improving Your State of Mind

People who have the same mindset as this apple orchard owner will find themselves to be very strong against the attacks of the demons of Hell. Even if they are in the same business, there are people who make various complaints and excuses about why they are not successful.

There are an infinite number of reasons that a farmer can come up with as to why he is unhappy. He can say, "The typhoon ruined months of my hard work," "It is the government's fault because they don't give us subsidies," "I am in this situation because my parents were farmers," or "It's God's fault for making typhoons come during this time of the year." Yet, people must not give up there. You must perceive the misfortunes as providence and think about how to cope with this situation for the best outcome. As you make efforts thinking in this way, great success will appear in front of you.

Since there are so many people in the world, it is impossible for everybody to be successful in a way that everyone is envious of. Each of you will meet plenty of failures and setbacks in your lifetime. However, when you do, I hope that you will remember that even if people are put in the same situation, there will be those that have the state of mind of a Bodhisattva, as well as those who have the state of mind of a demon in Hell.

In any setback or failure that you experience, find in it the Will of Heaven and do all that you can to open up a new path in your life. Even if you cannot change your surroundings, you can change your way of thinking and your state of mind to get over your setbacks.

I hope that you will take this lesson to heart and build within yourselves the ability to endure setbacks.

Have Courage and Break Out of Your Shell

When people become a little smarter,
They sometimes become indecisive.
Overly sensitive to the little things,
They start limiting themselves.
Making tidy excuses,
They explain why they cannot do something.

However
Developing these skills
Will do nothing for the world.

When you challenge new horizons
And work towards progress,
Do not think about the excuses why you cannot.
Always think about how you can.

Have courage and break out of your shell.
Take action.
Do not make excuses for why you cannot.
Instead, always ask yourself how you can.

Chapter III

Never Lose Your "Hungry" Spirit

Become a Different Person Through Continuous Studying

THE LAWS OF COURAGE

Chapter **III**

Never Lose
Your "Hungry" Spirit

1. Stay Young with a "Hungry" Spirit

Definition of the "Hungry" Spirit

Among the books that I have authored, there is a book called *The Origin of Youth* (original title: *Seishun-no-genten*, published by IRH Press) which focuses mainly on the topic of self-effort. In this chapter, I will reference *The Origin of Youth*, and offer discussions on the topic of "Never losing your 'Hungry' spirit" in the hope that I can offer something of value to the young, as well as to the middle-aged and elderly readers.

First, I will explain what I mean by a "hungry" spirit. Hungry is a feeling that you get when your body wants food. However, in this case, I am not using the word "hungry" in regards to a physical hunger, but rather a spiritual "hunger."

In the preface of *The Origin of Youth*, I stated, "This piece of work was toiled out of my soul, like the silk of a silkworm, when I was young, unknown and poor." The word "hungry" spirit is like a synonym for the words: young, unknown and poor.

Simply because of their age, young people are often taken lightly or looked down upon by adults. They are not taken seriously because there are only a few socially important people who are young. Additionally, young people, for the most part, have not made a name for themselves yet. There are only a limited number of famous young people, usually found within a small fraction of celebrities and athletes. Young people are also generally poor. Of course, some young people may have wealthy parents, but most students have limited finances and live at a moderately low level.

In that sense, young people may think of themselves as being "no ones" or "no-bodies." They are still "no-bodies," as they are "nothing" yet, and the society does not acknowledge them as full-fledged people. For that reason, young people have a hope and a strong desire to be recognized as independent adults. I am referring to this as the "hungry" spirit.

Never Give Up

Young people have a relatively easy time keeping a "hungry" spirit. This is because, just as people want to eat when they are hungry, young people want recognition and respect. They want to succeed, improve, and advance in life. They want to do a good job, and become the kind of adult who can guide others. Young people feel that they are lacking in a variety of ways. I think that this is the present circumstance of young people.

Those who are currently in their 30s, 40s, 50s or even older were also once young and with a "hungry" spirit. However, little by little, they start to lose those feelings of "hunger" that they had when they were young. Gradually, they accept the way things are as inevitable and give in to the flow of life. What is more, as they age, they begin to complain and make more and more excuses. Their main interests turn to illness and health problems, and they can no longer see their future.

In this way, as people grow older, they generally lose their "hungry" spirit. That is how life usually is. However, I wish you to maintain your "hunger" even when you are in your 30s, 40s, 50s or even 60s.

When people lose their "hungry" spirit, they cease to be "young." Whether people have this "hunger" is the deciding factor on whether they are youthful or not. It is a question of if they have the feeling of "not being satisfied with themselves yet," or "not feeling full yet." If you say it in another way, it is the spirit of never giving up. A person's youth exists in his or her determination to never give up.

The people who are determined not to give up are "young." People who declare that they can do something more and keep a "hungry" spirit, will always be young at heart, whether they are in their 40s, 50s, 60s, 70s or even 80s. However, most people tend to give up before reaching their goals. They become satisfied with the way things are, and let circumstances dictate their lives. Their lives become subject to the law of inertia. Living exactly in the way they have always lived, they never look to be any better than they are. They stop trying to reach the next level. They cease to try anything difficult, and they stop challenging themselves to new things. People who are in this state have lost their "hungry" spirit. I urge the elderly to recall what it was like to have that hunger. I would like for you to look back at what it was like to be young.

2. Three Perspectives That Will Help You Grow

The Relationship Between Your Brain and Stamina

Next, I will discuss how to retain your "hungry" spirit as you grow. First off, it is important to strengthen your brain and body, and increase your inner strength.

In chapter 1 of *The Origin of Youth*, titled "Aiming to be a 'Young Buddha'," I wrote, "It is important in your late teens and early twenties to strengthen your brain, body, and your inner strength, and develop job skills that are needed to become an adult."

The first point is to strengthen your brain. This is something that teachers are also teaching at school, so I assume that you are all doing this to a certain degree. The second point is to strengthen your body. Since this is something athletes or physical education teachers do, you may think that it has nothing to do with you. However, there is a relationship between strengthening your brain and strengthening your body.

It is normal for people in their early twenties to be active in both sports and academics. Since their bodies are strong, they do not see the relationship between these activities. Yet as they get older, they begin to understand that these two activities are closely related. It is normal to exercise and study when you are a student, so there should not be any problems. However, if you stop training your body after you start your career, there are times when your intellectual abilities will start to suffer. No one really teaches this, so I think there are many people who are unaware of this relationship.

Build Up Your Physical Strength

While in school, you are expected to exercise your brain and body and to do your best at both your studies and sports. This is actually the basic model for life. However, few people can keep up these habits after getting a job. When you start working, you will become very tired because of your work, and it is very difficult to continue exercising both brain and body in the time outside of work. Unless you have a great deal of endurance and will power, it is not something that you can keep up. Yet, I can say with confidence that those who try to maintain both their physical and intellectual activities will gradually separate themselves from the rest of the pack.

If after your twenties or thirties, you find that you are having a hard time reading books or that your work does not efficiently progress, there is a big chance that you are physically out of shape. If this is the case, you need to introduce some sort of exercise into your lifestyle.

When you are a student, your body is strong. In most cases, a night of sleep can restore your stamina, so you are a stranger to fatigue. The same goes for when your head is tired. Some young people might understand what it feels like when your head is tired, but most young people usually do not because it only takes a night of sleep to recover.

When I was young, I rarely felt that my head was tired. However, after a certain age, I became more familiar with that exhaustion that comes after studying for too long. I found that unless I got moderate exercise through walking or other physical activities, I could not make it through difficult books. It was impossible for me to continue studying without stretching and improving my blood circulation.

Do not think lightly of physical stamina, assuming that you do not need to think about your body because you have a job that uses your brain. Your intellect-related activities will come to a stop, and you will find yourself aging rapidly if you do not continue to build basic physical strength.

Balancing Study and Exercise

If you desire to stay young, it is vital that you regularly

exercise your body. However, it takes a great deal of determination to continuously balance both study and exercise. In that sense, the third aspect of increasing your inner strength connects to the increase of your physical strength and intellectual strength.

In most cases, people who are actively studying have a tendency to stop exercising, and people who exercise tend to stop studying. What is more, if they try to do both, they end up being average people. It is a very difficult choice that people face. If you focus solely on your studies, your body will suffer, and if you focus only on exercise, your grades will slip. However, if you try to do both, you will become an average person.

How do you escape this situation? Wisdom and will power can balance these seemingly incompatible opposites. At the start, you will need a great deal of will power. You must continue to encourage yourself as you train yourself. However, a little by little, what we can call the power of inertia, or the power of habit, will begin to work. You have reached a high level if through the power of habit, you are able to enjoy both exercise and study without feeling you are making an effort.

3. You Can Start a New Life at Any Age

A Career in Your Favorite Subject

Especially in the case of young people, their biggest worry is probably about their future career. I believe many young people in school worry about what type of career will bring them success, or what type of professional plan they should design for their future. Furthermore, since most of the subjects that students are studying do not directly apply to their desired professional field, they are often unsatisfied with their school's curriculum. They are frustrated because while they are studying subjects like English, math, science, social studies, and modern and classical literature, none of these subjects relate to any jobs, let alone their own career paths.

However, another perspective is possible. Regardless of the fact that all students in the educational system are studying similar curriculums, you will discover that there are subjects that you are good at and subjects that you are not. Therefore, it is possible to think that you are choosing your future career as you are studying at school.

In most cases, people are most suited for jobs that relate to their favorite subjects. The saying goes that you do best at what you enjoy, so it is safe to say that you are probably most fit for the type of work that you enjoy. For example, if you really like a foreign language and enjoy studying it, then your chances of succeeding in a job in which you use that language are very high. If you love math and find intellectual satisfaction in studying it, then it might be good for you to pursue a job in which you use math.

If there are people who did not do well in academics but are confident in their athletic ability, maybe they should look into a job that will use their body.

While you may be unsatisfied with the curriculum at your school, you should recognize that your future path will become clearer to you as you distinguish the subjects that you excel in from the ones you do not. Look at the balance between these subjects, and decipher for yourself upon which path your destiny lies.

Your Ability to Study and Your Future Job

When it comes to formal education, there are various paths. Some people go to technical schools to learn specific skills, some go to junior colleges, and some go to four-year universities. The difficulty level for acceptance into each school varies as well. When it comes down to it, the differences that become apparent between people in terms of education is that the harder the four-year university you attend, the more you can think in an abstract way. Four-year university students gain the ability to comprehend abstract concepts that cannot be physically seen or touched, and understand thoughts and systems formed by words that are not concrete.

Those who excel at their studies and attain a high level of education learn to comprehend abstract concepts. On the other hand, there are people who do not score so high on national standardized tests, university entrance exams, or on any of the wide variety of difficult tests offered, and do not attend the top schools. They may be more suited for concrete, down-to-earth jobs.

Those who are good at studying have a tendency

to go on to jobs that require abstract thinking such as researchers, government officials, and bankers. However, those who do not excel in their studies may find it easier to succeed if they narrow down their direction and focus their talents towards more down-to-earth jobs that deal with concrete goods or customers.

Studying Makes the Difference

The career choice that you make when you are 18 or 19 years old is no more than a preliminary decision, and you can start over new by choosing a different path at any time you want. Of course, it is possible to stir up a new resolve halfway through your life, and start on a different path.

For example, there may be people who hated their foreign language class in high school and found a job that had nothing to do with that language. Yet later on, they may start thinking that they would like to work overseas. Even if they start studying that language from the age of 30 or even 40, if they set their mind to it, there is still a chance to succeed. That is the power of

You can start over new
by choosing a different path
at any time you want.

studying. The difference is clear between the people who have studied and the people who have not.

About 140 years ago, Yukichi Fukuzawa (1834–1901) wrote a best selling book called *Gakumon no Susume* ('An Encouragement of Learning'). Fukuzawa teaches one thing through this book. He clearly states that all people are equal and that they are not ranked high or low by birth. The only difference between people is whether they have studied or not. He is saying that studying can make you a different person. He taught and encouraged the people of the Meiji period that if they study a certain subject, they can get a job in that field, and become a different person. Studying is what distinguishes one person from another. In a way, Fukuzawa's words live on to this day.

Fukuzawa also encouraged people to learn practical studies. By practical studies, he meant practical education or studies that you can use in this world. Foreign language is certainly an example of practical studies. Other than that, law, economics, commercial sciences, engineering, architecture and the study of constructing buildings and bridges are all examples of practical studies. I believe that Fukuzawa's encouragement of practical studies was an important educational movement.

Though I am a religious leader, I studied law and politics at my university. Normally, those who seek to become people of religion graduate with a degree in the field of liberal arts such as religion, philosophy or Indian Theology. However, I did not major in those fields. Even after entering the professional world in my twenties, I mainly studied practical subjects such as economics, business management, and international relations. I would use my time after work and my days off to study religion, ideologies, and about the spiritual world. Eventually, the content of those studies became my main line of work. That is why Happy Science has certain unique characteristics.

One of those characteristics is the backgrounds of the members. You will find that most of the members are not people who had religious backgrounds or people who like religion. Rather, most members are people who became involved with religion for the first time after they met the teachings of Happy Science.

Another characteristic is that while I certainly push faith forth very strongly, a rational mentality and the concept of making clear distinctions is quite evident in our religion. This is because I entered the religious world with a background of practical studies in this world. I am confident in my ability to look at the world, evaluate whether something is of value or not, and declare the worthless to be worthless. I believe that these characteristics make Happy Science unique from other religions.

4. Effort Invites Heavenly Powers

I Have Never Once Forgotten the Spirit of Self-Help

I founded Happy Science on October 6, 1986. At that time, there were only two volunteer staff members in a nine square meter room. Now, Happy Science has largely expanded its activities to all over Japan and is now spreading widely overseas.

Behind all this growth is, of course, the help of the guiding spirits and supporting spirits of Heaven. Great powers from the spiritual world are at work. Through this, our ability has been multiplied ten, twenty, and even a hundred times. Yet, that is not the only thing at work. I have published over 500 books and delivered countless lectures, and behind the scenes of my work, there is a vast accumulation of my own intellectual efforts.

For the past twenty some odd years, I have worked as diligently as I could. I received power from Heaven, but I have never depended completely on that power. From the time that I decided to dedicate myself to learning at the age of ten, through my fervent studies in my twenties, and to this day when I am over fifty years old, I have never once forgotten the spirit of self-effort and self-help. I have never forgotten that Heaven helps those who help themselves.

When you see someone making effort wholeheartedly, you naturally feel a desire to cooperate and support them. However, when you see a person who is lazy and slothful, or see someone who always tries to take the easy way out, do you feel like helping that person? Can you respect and support that person? The high spirits of

Heaven feel the same way. They want to help people who are always making effort and steadily working with all earnestness. The high spirits desire to support and to help these people become leaders.

Inspiration Comes to Those Who Make Effort

A foreign proverb says, "The devils tempt all, yet the idle man tempts the devils." In other words, the idle man seems as though he wants to walk the path of damnation so badly that he calls out the devil. The devils despise most the type of person who steadily works with diligence. The devils hate those who are humble, who work with untiring perseverance, and who steadily progress. These kinds of people are on a completely different wavelength from the devils.

In Happy Science, we teach people to discipline themselves and to always make effort. You may think that these are strict teachings, but these are ways to protect you from devils. These are also ways to receive the protection and support of the high spirits. This is one of the meanings of making effort. Devils cannot easily approach those who make effort to improve themselves. The high spirits always have the wish to guide these people and open a path for them.

One power that comes from the high spirits is inspiration. For example, entrepreneurs suddenly come up with new business ideas, inventors come up with new concepts for inventions, researchers stumble across clues to answers they have been searching for, and novelists come up with good stories.

In this way, inspiration will visit you and you will make various discoveries and observations within your jobs. However, inspiration comes most frequently to those who are already making efforts every day. There is the chance that inspiration will come to you once or twice in your life out of nowhere, but if you want to constantly receive inspiration, you will need to accumulate a lot of hard work behind the scenes.

Inspiration comes most frequently to those who are already making efforts every day.

5. A Study Method to Improve Your Life

From Schooling to Reading

I have discussed the spirit of self-help as it applies to the importance of learning. Next, I will speak to you about how to study.

First, though it is an orthodox method, when you are a student, it is important to properly attend to your studies at school. Teachers are teaching in a way they think is best after researching various teaching methods. So whether it is a regular school, a private tutoring school, or a prep school, for the most part, you should master the methods of that school.

After you graduate from your university or after you start your actual job, you will be able to choose what you read, so it is important to continue learning through reading. What you choose to read will have a great impact on the way you learn as an adult.

Meticulously Read Books in Your Field

At first, most people do not know what they should

read. They have no idea of what is good to read or what book will benefit them, and they wonder how they should pursue their post-school learning.

Since I was young, I have read about 1000 books per year. In chapter 7 of my book, *Talks on the Royal Road of Life*, (original title: *Jinsei-no-oudou-o-kataru*, published by IRH Press) titled "An Era of Daybreak," I wrote that the first step to enter the world of intellectuals is to read at least 1,000 decent books.

Upon hearing this, you may be saying to yourselves, "There is no way I can read 1000 books!" I read about 1000 books in a year so this number did not sound too difficult for me, but in reality, reading 1000 books seems to be quite a hurdle. Even when looking over the resumes of new staff members of Happy Science, most people have only read a few hundred books. Less than one out of every hundred applicants has read 1000 or more books.

Of course, when you are young, meticulous reading is generally important in your studies, so it is not critical to have read 1000 books while you are still a student. Typically speaking, school textbooks and reference texts need to be read carefully, so reading random pages or speed-reading will do you no good. This type of reading will not help you score better on your tests. The basic method of studying at school is to read carefully, take notes, solve practice questions, and meticulously read repeatedly as you underline important passages.

In order to form an intellectual foundation, meticulous reading is necessary. You simply have to study carefully and thoroughly. You will not learn anything by just flipping through the pages. If you want to succeed in a certain professional field, you must thoroughly study that field. If you do not dig your "well of knowledge" deep enough, you will never become one of the best in your field. You will never become a true professional.

Reading Widely to Expand Your Horizon

After you have dug your "well of knowledge" to a certain degree in your employed field, you should branch out into other topics and fields. It does not matter when, but spend some time during your breaks or days off reading about different fields. Little by little, read them for recreation when you want to change your mood. By reading books outside of your field, it will broaden your genre of knowledge.

As these books do not relate to your area of expertise, you do not need to study them as carefully. It is enough to get the general gist of what the author is saying, and pick up useful tidbits of information that you might need. As you do this, your reading speed will become faster and you will be able to read widely. If you read with the intent to simply collect bits of information here and there, your reading speed should pick up and you should be able to read quite a variety of books.

Balance Meticulous Reading with Wide Reading

However, indiscriminate wide reading will never lead you to be a truly well read person. People who read a wide variety of books in this way tend to lean towards books with very light subject matter. They are only able to read genres such as science fiction, mysteries, comics, or how-to books.

You must not let yourself read only books with light material. You will never become truly well read or truly educated unless you can balance wide reading and meticulous reading. However, meticulous reading and wide reading are two conflicting ways of reading, so it makes it difficult to do both.

Finding Books to Read Over and Over

In addition to reading at a very fast pace to obtain information in wide reading, you can also look for books that are worth reading repeatedly. Once you have read a certain number of books that you are interested in, you will be able to identify the ones you should read repeatedly. Until you actually read a good number of books, you will not be able to tell which books are worth re-reading. It is not that easy to determine at first whether a certain book is a masterpiece to you and is a necessity in your life.

Thus, a certain degree of wide reading is necessary when searching for books that are worth reading many times. If a certain book registers on your radar as a good book, you should read it over from time to time. Instead of re-reading it immediately, you should pick that book up again after a year or two, or after a few years. Through re-reading the same book, the lessons contained in that book will enter into your mind. After you re-read a book five to ten times, the ideas of the author will become your own as the thoughts sink deeply into you. Then, before you know it, the deep knowledge that has permeated into you will become a part of your inner power. You will see the influences of it when you are voicing your opinion or when you are making decisions.

Discoveries Within the Books of Truth

Among those books, I would like you to read the books of Truth multiple times. The Truth reveals the mind of Buddha and God, and the immutable rules that are common for all of mankind.

As a religious leader, I have preached the Truth and I have written many books. Therefore, if you are a fervent member of Happy Science, even if you are young, you probably have read a great number of books of Truth. If you are such a person, the words of Truth should naturally come out of you.

When people who are not familiar with the Truth hear those words, they should be impressed that you are quite capable and mature for such a young person. They will be awestruck by the fact that a person of merely twenty or thirty years of age is saying things that would usually only come out of someone who is an expert in life.

This is one of the fruits of re-reading the books of Truth many times. You cannot absorb the Truth in a single reading. However, if you repeatedly read these books with intervals of time in between, the contents will sink deeply and become a part of you.

Take for example, the book, *The Origin of Youth*. In its pages, I wrote what I call the secrets of success for people in their teens, twenties, and early thirties. Therefore, it would befit young people to pick this book up and re-read it from time to time. There are many times when a section you had skimmed over last time, jumps out at you during a subsequent reading. You will discover something different each time you read the book. By putting some time between readings, you will make new discoveries in accordance to your needs at that time.

I have not lived more than fifty years for nothing. I have identified and collected most of the pitfalls that young people fall into in the book, *The Origin of Youth*, and in other works that I wrote for the youth. However, because my writing style is simple, young people may overlook important points when reading these books. It is for this reason that I urge you to re-read these books after some time. You will be able to understand the meaning of the book when that knowledge becomes necessary for you.

Knowledge Supports Your Power to Influence

CEOs of large chain bookstores give their seal of approval to my books and even read them in their private lives.

As a modern religious leader, I believe that I have a diverse academic background. I also believe that one of the reasons that my religious activities have influenced such a wide range of people is because of this academic background. In actuality, I continue to influence many people who are not yet members of Happy Science. The background of this is the fact that I have been making effort. Because of that, I am able to receive support from Heaven.

By discussing the importance of self-effort and by presenting a way of self-development centered on intellectual training, this chapter has explored the topic of having a "hungry" spirit. By continuing to make tireless efforts, your intellectual ability will steadily increase, and it will stock up within you as your capability.

Do not lose your "hungry" spirit, no matter how old you become. I urge you to build in yourselves the courage to live your life powerfully through continuous intellectual training.

Chapter **IV**

Be Like a Roaring Fire

Discover True Courage by
Imagining the Last Moments of Your Life

THE LAWS OF COURAGE

Chapter **IV**

Be Like a Roaring Fire

1. People Who Succeed and People Who Fail

Unhappy People Only Think About Themselves

In this chapter, as I have titled "Be Like a Roaring Fire," I will talk about the mental preparations people need to make in order to succeed in this world. Though it is a very powerful title, I would like to speak not only for young people but also for the benefit of a wide range of readers.

First, most young people are probably concerned about their own self-realizations and their plans for the future. Perhaps they are uncertain of their future. When I was around the age of twenty, I was not extraordinarily outstanding, nor did I have an exceptionally higher state of mind compared to other people. As I reflect on my life, I feel that, in a sense, I had a very self-centered perspective of the world when I was a student. I will use the word "self-centric," but I feel that I had been living a life from only my point of view.

During their days as students, most people are probably living like this. 80 to 90% of all students cannot help but to think in a self-centric way. Only those who learned an ideology from their elders, or some line of teaching, philosophy, or religion in their childhood are able to hold a different perspective.

People who grew up in normal circumstances and lived among competitiveness are most likely living a self-centric way of life. They think, "What should *I* do? How do *I* succeed? How can *I* find self-realization?" These people only have interest in their own future, and are not concerned about others. Their own future, their own success, their own promotion; they are most likely spending all day thinking about themselves.

I was the same way, so I do not have the right to criticize young people. Like most young people, I also spent my time as a student thinking about myself. Of course, the time you spend as a student is the time to study. The studying that you do is for your knowledge. After your studies are completed, the knowledge you have acquired will give something beneficial and valuable back to society. That is why it is important to invest in yourselves and study for the advancement of yourself in your schooling years. There is nothing wrong with this at all.

However, I want to tell the young people that, in my case, when I thought only about my personal success, I was not able to become happy. During my school days, I pursued only my personal happiness and my own success, believing that I would never be happy if I was not successful. When I was a student, I was rather sensitive and was troubled by feelings of inferiority and jealousy.

Instability Comes from Not Being Acknowledged

The need to always put others down reveals just how unhappy a person is. Happy people rarely speak poorly of or criticize others.

There are people who slander others and say bad things about others. There are also people who put themselves down. These people feel that they are not recognized enough. The backlash of this feeling will result in one of two extremes: lashing out at others or abasing themselves.

The strong willed, competitive, or extroverted people tend towards the former action of attacking others. These types of people harm other people. Their abuse takes many forms such as insulting, taking advantage of others, criticizing, gossiping, ostracizing, excluding people, and plotting behind another's back. The actions they take may vary, but they basically bully other people.

On the other hand, quiet introverted people choose the latter action of tormenting themselves. This will begin with the feeling of inferiority. They may feel inferior because of their lack in intelligence, an unpleasant disposition, less-than-ideal looks or body, a poor family, or the parent's lack of social status. For these people, an infinite number of things make them feel inferior. Many people find every aspect of their inferiority to others and use them as excuses to defend themselves. They console themselves, dote in self-pity, and play the role of a tragic hero or heroine. By consoling themselves that they are tragic heroes, they feel as though they are saved. Great masses of people spend their lives sympathizing with their own unhappiness.

The third type of people constantly attacks both themselves and others at the same time. These people are naturally gifted and are generally strong willed, but they also have a sensitive side. When alone at home, they will harshly criticize themselves, feel hurt and cry. When out in public though, they insult and attack others, brag of their accomplishments and criticize others. They are very complicated people.

When you come across a person like this, your impression would probably be that the person is abusive and hard to get along with. Nevertheless, in reality, these people go home and weep bitterly, regretting their actions. They hate themselves to the point that they want to die. On a number of occasions, many young people probably feel that they want to crawl into a dark hole because they are so ashamed.

Making Others Happy Makes You Happy

I have discussed with you about different types of people, but I have personally experienced all of these emotions as well. It will become a story of the past as time passes by, but it can feel like an inescapable vortex for those of you whose minds are swaying back and forth between the two extremes right now. People who are within this storm of suffering must be having a very hard time trying to escape it.

I suffered for years while I was in my twenties, but then came to a simple awakening. This awakening was the conclusion of a long battle of mentality that I had fought in my twenties. Simply put, I realized that I would never find happiness or success as long as I focused on myself. As long as people hold a self-centric point of view and think, "*I* want to become happy," or "*I* want to succeed," they cannot become happy or successful.

I found the Truth that people become happy and successful when they decide to make others happy and help others succeed. While this Truth is very simple, this teaching is a part of all world religions. We call it the Golden Rule, and this Truth is always included somewhere inside each world religion.

Those who live self-centered lives have extreme difficulty realizing this simple Truth. Unless they experience a setback or adversity and open their eyes to the spiritual Truth, they are just not able to realize this. So, if I were to give you one bit of advice as you begin your professional careers, this would be it: *Be a person who brings happiness to others. Become a person who can bring success to others. This is the path to your success as well.* This Truth will be the deciding factor on whether you will become a success or a failure in the professional world.

Be a person who brings happiness to others.
Become a person who can bring
success to others.
This is the path to your success as well.

People Who Bring Happiness to Others Will Succeed

Since these words are abstract, let me try to illustrate it with specific examples. This concept does not pertain only to geniuses or other great men and women. It holds just as much truth for people in regular careers in any type of job.

Take, for example, a comic book artist. The artist who draws hoping to please a wide audience will succeed. On the other hand, the artist that only draws what he or she wants to draw will not succeed. This principle pertains to taxi drivers too. Most customers are pressed for time. The driver who will drive the customer accurately and dependably to their destination every single time will be successful.

The same holds true for schoolteachers as well. Successful teachers are people who rack their minds about how they can help each individual student foster their strengths while helping them overcome their weaknesses. They also think about how the students can grow up healthy. Teachers who are able to guide the students by truly thinking about each one of them will be successful.

Some teachers only think about getting through each day, so all they do is waste time during class. It is very unlikely that these useless teachers will become happy. The phrase "killing time" describes this quite accurately. "Kill" is a harsh word, but some teachers are indeed "killing" time.

Successful teachers look at all of their students and hold in their hearts that teaching this unique class is a "once-in-a-lifetime-chance." Teachers who believe that their class is special and wish to teach the class something valuable or meaningful will be successful.

The same holds true for jobs in companies or corporations. Let us say that you are in sales and you have benchmarks to reach. Whether you are a salesperson at a department store or you work at a jewelry store, someone always sets benchmarks for your daily, monthly, and yearly sales that you have to reach. However, there is a big difference between the person who works hard just to meet the quota and the person who works hard to make others happy.

Let us say, for instance, that you get a job at a

department store and you join the women's clothing department. Regardless of the fact that you are a new employee, you have daily, monthly and yearly sales goals. However, you cannot tell your customer about your quota. You cannot say to your customer, "I have a sales goal of 5,000 dollars today, so please buy the remaining 2,000 dollars so I can reach my sales goal." Of course, no customer is going to buy from you simply because you have 2,000 dollars left to reach your 5,000 dollars goal. Everyone would simply walk away without buying anything. Customers could not care less what the sales associate's benchmarks are. Sales figures only pertain to the income and career advancement of that individual.

Now, successful people in the exact same women's clothing department would have an entirely different focus. They would look at their customer and put extra care into thinking about what type of clothing would make their customer look good, or about what clothes would bring out her natural charm. They would consider what kind of clothing would make their customer more lovable to her husband or boyfriend.

They would think about what type of clothing would look attractive on their customer. These sales associates would try to imagine what type of jewelry would look good on their customer. People who succeed are those who make these notions of care or mindfulness to others.

Being successful or not comes down to a single thought. Those that are self-centered will not succeed. It is the other way around. Those who have the success of other people in their minds will succeed themselves.

Another example of this is in the culinary world. Whether they are cooking in restaurants or at home, chefs who work as chefs just for the purpose of making a living will not succeed. Chefs, who put their hearts into their wish for customers to become healthy, nourished and energized, will be successful. Whether they are serving customers or cooking in the kitchen, those who earnestly wish that the children dining at the restaurant will grow up strong and that the family will enjoy their dinner together, will happily walk the path of success.

However, there are chefs who blame the head chef

for not teaching them how to cook, and unwillingly cook their dishes. Usually in the culinary world, most experienced chefs do not teach their apprentice chefs how to "cook well." They tell their apprentices to steal the recipes, flavors, and soups of others on their own. The apprentices learn the ways of cooking over the years by observing how other chefs prepare their dishes, by stealing a taste, and by watching how the other chefs combine the spices and flavorings. There are kitchens where the head chefs do not kindly teach their apprentices how to cook. There may be even kitchens where the head chef will punish the apprentices when they cannot learn on their own. In these working situations, if you can only conceive yourselves as being bullied at work, you will not be successful.

On the other hand, people who make it their own purpose to seek the ways they can bring happiness to their customers will succeed without doubt. The most important essence of all of this is actually in this one point. *The road that leads to the happiness of others not only brings happiness to others, but will also bring happiness to you.* I hope that you will always keep this in the corner of your mind. It is a simple way for you to find success.

Discover a Future Within Yourself

People have a tendency to live with a self-centric perspective and live a self-centered life. This is an important reason why you should change your way of thinking, and keep an attitude that will help others succeed and find happiness. When you are able to see from this point of view, the doors to gaining recognition in your career will start to open. I would like to emphasize strongly that this is the way to achieve self-realization.

One more thing is that even though each person will enter his or her own path of happiness and will start to become successful, it does not mean that everybody will walk the same path. Since every person is born with different gifts and talents, the path that each person will follow will differ from one another.

In Happy Science, we teach that it is important to study hard, but that does not mean everyone will do exceptionally well in studies. Not everyone will be brilliant students and become scientists, executives, bankers, or lawyers. You are supposed to enter various professions, and it is extremely important that you first know your potential.

You must find your future within yourselves. It is very important to discover the image of your future self within your own mind. What kind of seedling of the future is sprouting inside of you? I would like you to discover this.

Learn from Everybody

The idea that graduates from top universities are superior and graduates from no-name universities are inferior seems to be widespread in this world. Society also views some careers as more superior than other careers. Please make effort to not look at the world through this perspective. Every person has his or her strengths, and there is something to learn from every person.

The writer Eiji Yoshikawa (1892-1962) seems to have lived by the words, "Everyone but I is a teacher." Even in his novel, the character Musashi Miyamoto says something to the meaning of "Everyone and everything in this world are teachers to me." This perspective of "Everyone but I is a teacher" is correct in a way.

In your classrooms, there are those who do not score as high on tests as you but are able to point out your mistakes, praise you for your strengths, and give words of guidance to you. There are also people considered to be at the bottom of the so-called food chain who say cutting remarks that are eye opening. You can learn so many things from the variety of people you meet in this world.

As you go out into the professional world, you will continue to meet many people such as your bosses, colleagues or friends, and there is something to learn from all of them. Therefore, you must not judge people on a matter of personal preference. It is important to think that all people have strengths and that you can learn from them. There may be people who you do not like or people who you do not want to become like. Maybe they have unattractive weaknesses or shortcomings. If you feel this way about someone, you should simply decide to not become like that person.

Observe their weaknesses and shortcomings, and if you find yourself repelled by them, it is important to tell yourself that you will not become like that, and make sure you actually do not.

However, in the decades that I have spent in the society, I have observed one thing. There are always people who say that they do not like a certain person or that they do not want to become like that certain colleague. Yet, when that certain colleague transfers to a different department, they start acting in the same ways as that colleague.

For example, victims of bullies end up picking on others. It would be great if they decide to praise others, but instead, they end up doing the exact same thing as the person they had hated. The reason this happens is that the ability to clearly see a certain fault in a person is usually a good indication that you share quite a bit in common with that person. It is because you and that person are so alike that you notice his or her shortcomings. If you had nothing in common with this person, you would not notice that person's faults. You see those faults clearly because you share similar characteristics with that person. That is why people who say, "I will never end up like that," often end up acting exactly like the people they had despised.

2. Become Good Leaders That Accomplish Great Work

Shine Like a Star in Your Twenties

Next, I will talk about which direction you should develop yourself in order to succeed. In your twenties, it is important to polish yourself and become a person that shines like a star.

Talented people are like "spikes in a cloth pouch." If you put a spike in a cloth pouch, the pointed end of the spike will punch through the cloth. Similarly, the talents of the bright and ingenious will eventually come to light, no matter where they are.

Those who show their talent instantaneously like "spikes in a cloth pouch" will look as though they are shining. These types of people are more likely to catch the eyes of their superiors, so they are supported, chosen, and look as though they are set on the path to success. This is what people in their twenties may experience. Unless you become someone that can radiate light, you will have a hard time being recognized by the people around you.

Leaders Nurture Others

As a sharp spike stabs people, if you are constantly hurting others by pointing out their failures or gouging out their weaknesses, you will never be able to do great work. This "spike in the cloth pouch" must grow into a person of high caliber. You must not use your strong intellectual skills only to hurt others. If you become a leader, no matter whom you are working with, you must make effort to help them grow in the way that corresponds with their skills.

For example, you should guide those with great talents to become even greater. Though there may only be a few, you should help prodigies develop their talents and lead them towards a higher goal. You should also cultivate the strong points of average people and help them overcome their weaknesses. If there are people with work skills below average, make efforts to bring them up to the standard level. It is very important to adjust the way you teach and nurture people according to the needs and characteristics of each individual person you work with.

Another important point is to bring people together through teamwork. It is a valuable experience to bring together a group of people, form a team and accomplish a single project or plan.

Leadership ability plays a huge role. You cannot measure the skill of leadership through a school exam. Leadership is the ability to pull five, ten or even more people together and make a big project happen. You can never measure this ability on a test in school. This ability only emerges once you enter the professional world. Whether the leadership potential in you comes to fruition or not is dependent largely on how open your mind is, your level of tolerance, and what caliber a person you are.

It is not merely about projecting your talents outwards or thinking only about developing your own abilities. Remember that all people have their own unique characteristics, and that you need to help develop every individual person in distinct ways that fit that person. It is important to head in the direction of improving the overall productivity of the group while keeping this in mind. That is what is required of a good leader.

I hope that you will always remember what I have shared with you in the back of your mind.

Key Points for Women to Become Good Leaders

In the future, more and more women will hold higher positions in the business world. Therefore, there are a few things that I would like for women to keep in mind when they move to higher positions.

About five or ten years after a woman enters a profession and starts having people working under her, a certain "law" will start to function. For one thing, women tend to be very strict when it comes to other women who work under them. No one has clearly stated this law, but it actually exists. When viewed from a different side, this law also points out that, women managers have a tendency to not praise other women who are younger than they are. This is a big difference between men and women. Men do not mind having women working under them. Yet, women are extremely hard on women subordinates, and they especially do not praise the younger women. This law exists in reality, so please be careful.

As a woman, if you find yourself in a position where you are in charge of others, please praise your female subordinates. This is the first major obstacle that women will encounter before being able to rise to a managerial position. Even from the perspective of men, there are many talented, hardworking women. Nevertheless, it is this obstacle, the question of whether she can get the most out of her female subordinates, that tips the scales one way or the other. Her boss is more worried about her ability to use her female subordinates than her ability to use her male subordinates.

The hardest task for women is to be able to use other women. The worst form of teasing happens between women. Men, in turn, are overwhelmed by this relentless relationship and have a hard time appointing women to management positions.

If you are a woman and are put in a managerial position, you must not pick on younger women simply because they are younger. It is important that you care for them. When you enter into a management position, you have to evaluate your subordinate's work in a fair, neutral and reasonable way. At the same time, you need to praise and appreciate them as they deserve, and develop in yourselves the desire to help your subordinates gain experience and become better workers. Even if you are still young and cannot imagine yourself in a management position yet, you should remember this point because you are prone to follow this tendency when you do become a manager. When you have younger female subordinates, do not pick on them just because they are young.

A woman in the workplace who is capable of giving credit to other women will find herself well thought of by her male colleagues. Companies feel comfortable in entrusting management positions to this type of woman. If you are this type of woman, your boss will understand your ability to use other women and will be able to promote you without worries.

Even if you are capable and talented as an individual, if you cannot use other people well, you will cause the team to fall apart and stop everyone from working efficiently. Since this causes an overall negative outcome, companies are not able to give you a promotion to a managerial position.

Now is a generation with many women leaders. Therefore, if you are a woman, you should strive to acquire the ability to make fair and equitable judgments. In order to judge people fairly, you should make effort to observe the work and skills of others from a neutral perspective.

You cannot expect special treatment as a woman. If you want to work in the professional world with men, you are going to have to be able to make fair and neutral judgments.

Advise for Men Working Under Female Managers

In the future, there will be many men working for women as well. It will be a time when many men will find themselves in a position where they are working under women managers.

What should you do when you are working under female managers? There are certain things that you are going to need to do. First, you should freshen up and dress neatly. Then you should make sure you fulfill all promises that you make, and completely carry out all the instructions that you receive.

Women absolutely hate unpolished, sloppy men who are not punctual. Women have these characteristics, so it is necessary that you make the effort to not physically disgust your female managers. You should be careful of this point when you are working under women.

In addition to this, never assert the perception of male superiority, and ridicule your boss because she is a woman. You must acknowledge her skills, be respectful, and be loyal to her as your boss.

If you keep this stance, you will be treated fairly by your boss. Remember that the company placed your boss in her position because she has the ability and skills necessary to be there. She undoubtedly has the ability, so if you are fair and neutral towards her, she will judge your work fairly as well.

3. Create the Second Renaissance

Now I would like to talk about a vision of the future that will be the dream and hope for young people. I have spoken about this several times in the past, but this era right now is the turning point of the grand span of history. The civilization that emerged in Greece moved westward to the United States, and flowed into Japan. Likewise, the Eastern civilization, which originated in India, traveled to China, and flowed into Japan.

Looking at the flow of history from a large perspective, one can see that now in Japan, a vast new civilization that unites both Eastern and Western civilizations is about to be born. As the Eastern and Western civilizations have flowed into Japan, the era will soon come when the new civilization emerging in Japan will flow outwards to the world. This is what I anticipate. That is why I hope that the young people who are going to live in this new era will create the second renaissance in Japan.

In order for this to happen, Japan must prosper and flourish in the 100 years of the 21st century as a country that leads the world. Starting with the government, the economy and art, the technological field including development in aerospace or advancements in oceanic studies, Japan must take leadership in every field of study. That is the life mission of young people living in Japan now.

If a new civilization that reaches new heights is created, many people from around the world will gather to Japan to study this new civilization. As water naturally flows from high grounds to low grounds, this new civilization will flow to all corners of the Earth. In order to create a new culture or a new civilization, there must be a spiritual foundation. It is necessary to have spiritual progress that measures up to the material progress. That is why I am giving many lectures of the Truth. I call this new civilization that we must progress towards, "The El Cantare Civilization."

Please, I wish for you to have great aspirations.

People will become what they think will become.

Your aspirations determine who you will become.

Show us your aspirations.

Then, you will know who you are.

You cannot rise above your aspirations.

Please take that into your hearts.

4. Have Courage and Live Like a Roaring Fire

You need courage in order to create a new era. Even if I told you to have courage, you may not know what to do. Some of you may be confused about what kind of person you should become. Think of courage as something that rises up when people prepare themselves for death.

There is a term "lay down your life for the Dharma" in Buddhism. It means to willingly give your life and to prepare yourself for death. Only when you are prepared to die for a cause will you realize what courage actually

People will become
what they think they will become.
Your aspirations determine
who you will become.

is. Only at this point, will you understand the nature of courage and be able to summon up true courage.

If you truly wish to know what courage is,
Ponder not on "how to live," but rather on "how to die."
Please ask yourselves and contemplate,
What kind of life do I want to live and how do I want to die?
How do I want my last moments to be?
What kind of human being do I want to die as?
After I die, how do I want people to remember me?

The answer to those questions is the courage that you need to have. I will say it again. *If you want to know what courage is, prepare yourself for death. At that instant, you will know the true nature of courage.* When you find the answer to those questions, true courage -like a roaring fire- will start gushing out from within you. From this point on, a brand new life will open in front of you.

Lastly, I am asking something from everyone, especially from those who are in their teens and twenties. Most of you will be on this Earth longer than I. Many of you may live to see the doors of the 22nd century about to open.

I wish you to convey my words to the youth of the 22nd century. Tell them that Ryuho Okawa told you that if you truly wish to know what courage is, prepare yourself for death. At this instant, you will know the true nature of courage.

The next century will bear a generation of youth of its own. That generation of youth will continue to build the new era towards the creation of the El Cantare Civilization. In order to convey the new youth of this aspiration to create the new civilization, those who are in your teens and twenties now must make it through this century.

Please live a bold and powerful life in order to open the path for the new era.

Destiny Will Take Care of Itself If You Have Courage

Destiny will take care of itself if you have courage.
If you have courage, anything is possible.
Stop making excuses and fight with courage.

If you have courage,
You will be able to say that one word.
If you have courage,
You will be able to extend a helping hand.
If you have courage, you can stand up strong.
If you have courage, you can save lives of others.
You will be able to change your own fate.
You will be able to change the fate of others.
This is what courage is.

Creating a Utopia begins with courage.
If no one stands up with courage
Utopia will never be realized.
There needs to be people
Who will willingly give their lives for this fight,
Who do not think about harvesting
For themselves,
And who do not wish to pick the ripe fruits
For themselves.
There needs to be people
Who will devote themselves
For the future generation.
Courage is what these people need.

Chapter V

Live a Life of Truth

*The Future Will Change
When You Realize Your Connection
to the Cosmic Tree*

THE LAWS OF COURAGE

Chapter V

Live a Life of Truth

1. A Perspective from the Cosmic Tree

A Massive Tree of Life Exists in the Universe

In this book, I have discussed many concrete ways of thinking about courage in life. In this last chapter, I would like to take a step forward into more mystical aspects of life and talk about the courage needed to fulfill a life of Truth. In the second chapter, I said that if you change your perspective, all of your suffering would start to look different. In this chapter, I would like to take that perspective to the broader level of the universe. What I would like to present now is a new outlook on humanity, on life, and on the world.

Ever since my spiritual eyes had opened nearly 30 years ago, I have continued to research the spiritual world. This new outlook on humanity and on the world is quite different from the common knowledge of society today. So please do not try to understand it based on this knowledge but rather, replace your old knowledge with this new outlook.

First, let us contemplate the meaning of your life. How do you understand the existence of *you* or *yourself*? You may believe that you are living your life as an individual human, and because you and others have separate bodies, everybody has an independent life. Yet, I would like everyone to consider whether this way of self-recognition is correct from the true perspective and outlook of life.

In the world of religion, there are many legends about a massive tree that exists in the universe. These legends have been passed down since the ancient times, and they say that there is a tree known as the Tree of Life growing in the universe. I wrote about a part of this secret in Chapter 5, "Living for Eternity" of my book, *The Laws of Life*, so there may be some of you who have read it already.

The world you would see through a telescope is much different from the world you would see with a spiritual eye. In this universe, there is in fact, a single massive tree that exists. The branches of this tree repeatedly divide as they extend into all different directions.

This Tree of Life is also called the Cosmic Tree. I am not the only one saying this. Though no one has ever seen it with his or her own eyes, this is a legend that has been passed down from a very long time ago. (As Scandinavian countries have the legend of the "World Tree," Mesopotamia, ancient China, ancient India, Mesoamerica and many other countries from all around the world also have numerous myths that reflect the image of the Tree of Life.)

El Cantare is the Root of All Life on Earth

Looking from a bigger perspective, you would see that the branches of this massive tree extend far beyond the level of this Earth and to all parts of the universe.

If you look at it from the point of view of the Earth,

it appears to be one big tree growing like a pillar within the terrestrial spirit group. El Cantare is the name of this immense Tree of Life, and this existence is the origin of all life on earth. All spiritual energy flows from here. There are many large boughs growing from this enormous Tree of Life, and these large boughs are actually the different ethnic groups. The various ethnicities from the different countries are equivalent to these boughs.

What is the factor that determines an ethnic group? It is religion. The differences between ethnic groups are actually the differences between religions. Ethnic groups were originally groups of people formed by individual religious leaders who had preached new teachings. Many large boughs had split off as the various religions and ethnic groups flourished in many different eras. In this way, religion exists at the fundamental basis of culture and civilization. During thousands of years, a certain ethnic group creates a culture that has various characteristics. People reincarnate there several times while experiencing the culture of that specific religion.

If you look towards the tip of this large thick bough

of an ethnic group, you can see it dividing repeatedly into smaller branches. There are cases in which each branch represents one country. There are also cases in which a branch goes beyond a country and includes various regions, such as certain regions in Asia or Europe. Another case would be that these individual branches spread throughout the world. These branches are segmented and extend to separate countries, regions or to various groups of people who share a certain way of thinking.

You Are a Part of the Cosmic Tree

The branches of the Cosmic Tree divide one after another. The large boughs split up into many medium sized branches, which divide into even smaller branches. At the tips of these small branches, there are an innumerable number of even thinner branches, which seem abundant with leaves. If you look at them even closer, at the tip of one of the smallest branches, there are about six leaves attached to it. These groups of six leaves that grow at the tip of the branch are seen as one life form, and these groups are called "soul siblings."

As a rule, a group of soul siblings consists of the core soul, which is the head, command tower, or the center of the soul, and five other soul siblings. This group of six souls together comprises one life form. Each soul takes turns being born on Earth. When the soul returns to the spiritual world after dying, most of them will keep the same appearance as when they were living on Earth. Even though each soul looks different, the core soul and branch souls are aware that they form one personality as a whole, and that they are all a part of one unique human soul.

Each soul has its differences including the differences in the outer appearance since everybody keeps the appearance of themselves in the various eras in which they were born. However, if you look at them as a whole soul and see them as one collective personality, you will see the memories and experiences of each soul overlapping in various cross sections.

As an example, let us say you were born in the Edo Period (1603-1867), Kamakura Period (1185-1333), and the Heian Period (794-1185) and you have the life experiences and appearances in your memory for every era in which you reincarnated into this world. If you were to show this process as a movie, corresponding to every reincarnation cycle, it would look as though there were many individuals. In this way, every human soul has the energy of about six people. The energy of about one sixth of the soul enters a human body, and he or she is born on Earth. Then after a few decades of spiritual training, they return to the other world with a new personality.

Everyone who is alive now will gain new experiences in this era of the 20th and 21st century, study new materials and return to the other world with new nourishments of life. Your soul siblings will share this new memory. In your soul, there are memories from a long, long time ago, but those memories gradually fade away as you are reborn in new eras and acquire new knowledge and experience.

The True View of Life

This view of life is the true view of life. It is quite different from the education that you receive at school or the information acquired from reading books and magazines, or watching television. In fact, most people will say that they have never heard of such thing. However, this view of life is the Truth and it is how the world actually is.

Your physical body existing right here right now is not your true self. Your true self is much like a traveler that happens to be visiting this finite sphere called Earth, which is only a small existence in this vast universe. As a traveler, you will stay here for a few decades but you will return to the other world after your visit. The purpose of coming to this world is to learn new lessons and obtain new knowledge.

Once you know this true perspective of life and of the world, you will completely reverse the way you view things. From your own point of view, you may think, "This is my real self. This individual that exists now is my real and only self, and everyone else is a separate person from me." You may have never heard from or seen the other world. You may have never heard about people coming back from the other world. You may not know where you came from or where

Your true self is much like a traveler
that happens to be visiting
this finite sphere called Earth,
which is only a small existence in
this vast universe.

you will go after this life.

This attitude is normal for this world, and we seldom learn any other view of life, even in our education system. Only true religions can teach you the real view of life and of the world.

2. Soul Mate: A Hint to Figure Out the Meaning of Life

Soul Mates and America's New Age Movement

As I explained in the last section, the massive Cosmic Tree divides repeatedly, and the various individuals exist at the very tips of these branches.

Accordingly, your soul exists at one of these tips. Now if you follow your tip of the branch up, you would see that there are several small branches much like yours, growing from the same big branch. These small branches are your soul mates, and they are souls that have been created around the same time as you. These souls are all related to you.

The word "soul mate" commonly appeared in a new

spiritual movement called the New Age Movement, which occurred in America during the 1970's. This so called "New Century Movement" or "New Era Movement" was popular in America, and the movement runs almost in parallel with the activities of Happy Science.

The backdrop to the popularity of this movement is that people feel that Christianity, taught as a traditional religion by the church, is no longer providing what people are seeking. Many people long to know more about the spiritual Truth. For this reason, people who seek answers to their troubles would go to people who can see and talk to spirits, or to people who can conduct readings of your past lives. By going to these people with spiritual abilities, they ask about the people that are close to them, such as spouses, parents, friends, business partners or other people who they have important relationships with. They ask about what kind of people they are, or what kind of spiritual relationship they have with them. In this New Age Movement, there are much activities focusing on these spiritual consultations.

Case 1: People Close to You
People with Spiritual Ties are Around you

These New Age groups have never grown as large as a religion like Happy Science, and a single group usually only has about a hundred to at most a thousand people. Nonetheless, spiritual phenomena occurred in many places and these life consultations became popular through this movement.

Christianity does not teach the view of the spiritual world or any spiritual knowledge, so people who want to know the Truth go to these New Age groups to ask if there is indeed something spiritual that exists.

What you basically learn from these consultations is that when you look at your previous lives, people you are having complications or conflicts with now are actually people that have been in many different human relationships with you throughout various reincarnations.

For example, even if you are husband and wife now, you may have been parent and child in a previous life. Perhaps in a previous life you were husband and wife, but you may now be father and daughter. Sometimes an older brother that you dearly love was actually your father in a previous life, or the uncle that is close to you and always gives you advice was actually your father in a past life.

Case 2: Divorce and Remarriage
Spiritual Ties in Remarriage

In the West, there are many divorces and remarriages. The New Age groups who give spiritual consultations advise people in these events as well. These people from the New Age groups answer questions about whether the person you plan to remarry is someone connected to you by fate. They also do readings of your past lives to see whether your new partner is someone close to you from a previous incarnation.

In Christianity, when two people marry, they pledge that no one shall ever separate what God has made one, so they feel guilty when they break that oath, divorce, and remarry. The church cannot rescue them from those feelings of guilt. Therefore, they search for a different perspective and seek a replacement for their religious salvation. When people hear that the person they are about to remarry has deep connections of fate according to these spiritual readings, those feelings of guilt disappear.

The answers that the life consultations of the New Age Movement provide are correct to some degree. In these modern times where people repeatedly divorce and remarry, there are many cases where the partner of the remarriage also has some connection of fate with you.

In my book, *The Laws of Life*, I wrote that you should not torment yourself over the red string of fate. Since there are so many divorces and remarriages in this unsettled flow of modern society, the concept of a single red thread of fate connecting two people as husband and wife no longer makes sense. Even if you find yourself experiencing divorce or remarriage, please do not think too gravely about this. The people who you have made a new spiritual tie with most likely had a spiritual tie with you in your previous lives.

Case 3: The Help of Soul Mates
Close Souls are Always Supporting Your Life

Currently the world population is above six billion, and it is growing towards seven billion people. It is almost certain that many different people from all different eras are being born all at once today.

In almost every era, you have a group of close souls that come to Earth with you for soul training. Many people of the same group are born in the same era with you. So if your relationships with family, friends, or business partners ever collapse completely, there will always be soul mates or soul friends that have spiritual ties with you that appear among your new relationships you make. In most cases, these soul mates will step out to help you.

A life span already lasts as long as 80 to 90 years these days, so I am sure that there is a wide variety of things that can happen in life. Please do not think of fate as something fixed or immovable. Please know that there are always friends of your soul or soul mates, who are supporting your life.

I believe you will meet someone in your lifetime that especially captivates your heart. This does not happen just between men and women, but also happens between women or between men. Even though they are not your relatives, you feel as though they are close family members. You may gain a lifelong friendship with someone who feels like a destined friend. Maybe you become Dharma Friends with the person who guided you to the teachings of the Truth, and you spend decades together. There are these types of connections, and soul mates actually do exist.

There may be people struggling to rebuild their lives or people who are amidst a huge swirl of guilt. Yet, please know that life is not that simple. Being born in various periods, you play different roles as you reincarnate repeatedly. Constantly switching roles in relationships, people are always going through life training.

It is possible that the person who is your mother now was actually your child at some point. It is also possible that the people you are rivaling with now were actually your siblings in your previous life. When you want to figure out the meaning of life, you must think about it to a much deeper level.

Now that you are aware of this Truth, when you meditate, I would like for you to think of a person that has made a strong impression in your life and think about whether that person has a special connection to your soul through fate.

Case 4: People You Always Encounter
Soul Mates as a "Workbook of Life"

I think that there is a group of about 20 to 30 people close to you who are all spiritually tied. This group of people actually decides and will most likely determine the happiness and unhappiness of your life. In almost all cases, you have met these people because you had planned to meet in this life.

In your life training, there are people who you are required to meet. Because of this arrangement, you will certainly meet these people at least once in your lifetime. Some people will treat you with the warmest kindness, but some will teach you with strictness or provide you with a trial in life. Nonetheless, they are the ones whom you absolutely must meet. This is in a sense a "workbook of life." You must meet certain people as a part of the workbook, and solve the issues you had with them in your past lives. You carried over assignments from your previous lives, and you must solve them in this lifetime.

For example, in a past life, you may have had a great relationship as a parent and child, brother and sister, or husband and wife. Yet, through the course of life, something happened between the two and you became to hate each other. In these cases, you must meet again in this lifetime in a different relationship to test how you will treat the other.

In most cases of love-hate problems that arise in relationships, especially when the relationships are with people who have a deep influence on your life, they are problems carried over from a past life. This problem from the workbook of life is a problem you must solve, and it is a part of God's plan for you. Please do not think you are facing suffering because you just happened to have bad luck. It is better to think that that you received a problem from the workbook of life. I would like you to know that many things happen because they are necessary and inevitable.

3. Erasing Hatred from Earth

Teachings of Love are Crucial in Individualist Societies

Without knowing this true perspective of life, it is very likely that you will live on thinking you are individuals that are completely isolated from each other. Many people follow the western values of individualism, believing that individuals who compete and win are superior, and think that you must defeat everyone or you will be defeated. They may waver between joy and sorrow over winning or losing, and their hearts may sway back and forth between a heavenly state of mind and a hellish state of mind.

Yet in actuality, one massive Tree of Life spreads largely through space and far beyond the realms of this Earth, stretching its branches to the other planets with life. There is a single great tree in the universe, and it connects all of the souls. You may compete to win or lose in this competitive society, but remember that your opponents are not your absolute enemies or rivals. They are people who you have met many times

185

through numerous reincarnations. I would like you to know that this single great tree spiritually connects us all.

This is why I am teaching to love. Please love one another. You must love each other. I am saying this because you are not strangers to each other. You have met each other many times in various eras and regions. Every single person is connected. Everybody's life energy connects to the same root of life.

Spiritual Ties Go Beyond Eras

In an era like this, when new teachings of the Truth are taught, many people with spiritual ties have reincarnated with you. Everyone was alive in the numerous civilizations of the past including the ones that are known as legends in the modern times. You have met each other in the era of King La Mu of the Mu civilization, in the era of Thoth, the great leader of Atlantis, in the era of Hermes in Greece, and in the era of Buddha in India. You had met each other repeatedly in different situations with different appearances, sometimes switching genders and switching roles

Please love one another.
You must love each other.
I am saying this because
you are not strangers to each other.
You have met each other many times
in various eras and regions.

within families. You should have met these people in this lifetime as well. There should be many life dramas taking place within all of this. In this context, I would like you to know that you have a deep connection with the people you meet. That is why I tell you to love each other.

Overcome Hatred and Unite the World with Love

The people you have close relationships with are all connected to the same branch of the Tree of Life. It is a sin to hate or loathe each other. It is a sin because you would be loathing, damaging, and trying to cut off another branch that is connected to the same bough of life as you.

People often say that jealousy and hatred exist at the opposite end of love, but I would like you to overcome this. You compete and grow jealous of people because you think you are completely separate from them, but they are actually fellow soul mates. In many cases, the person that you despise or hate has an extremely deep spiritual tie with you, and is someone you have met many, many times in your previous lives.

This is why I tell you, "Stop hurting each other. Stop speaking badly of each other. Do not be jealous of others but bless them instead, and you will be able to develop your own soul too." When individualism becomes overly strong, it leads to a strong expression of jealousy, possessiveness, and hatred. Looking from the viewpoint of the Tree of Life, this is equivalent to allowing your own leaf to wither, or chopping off your own branch on the Tree of Life. This goes against the laws of life, and it will be judged as a hellish deed that requires self-reflection.

I am teaching you that everyone is an existence that originally branched off from one immense Cosmic Tree. So please love each other. Everybody comes from the same root. Today, so much hatred and conflicts are born because of the differences in race or religion, but that is only because they do not understand this Truth. If we understand that we are actually all branches from the same tree, war and hatred will have to vanish from this Earth. The purpose of the movement of Happy Science is to teach this to everybody. In this regard,

Happy Science is trying to unite the world. We are trying to bring peace and abundance to this world in the truest sense.

4. Living with Faith Above All

A Reversal of the Value System

Human beings, each one of us, are existences that have branched off from the Tree of Life. You are one part of the six soul siblings that was born on this Earth for soul training to gain new experience and knowledge. Because people do not understand the outlook of life from a much larger perspective, the values have been reversed in this world. Everybody's thoughts are based on the logic built on specialized individual knowledge.

For instance, there are intellectual doctors who become fixated on materialism. There are also teachers that believe that they cannot participate in any religious activity, or mention anything about faith since they are public workers. Teachers should fundamentally be "teachers of souls," but many believe that they should not read, listen, or acknowledge anything related to religion, and should deny all religious teachings. Many teachers have this attitude and act on it without a strand of doubt. These kinds of things should not happen. There are so many things happening in today's society that are wrong from the perspective of the true morals of life, the laws of life, and the ethics of good and evil.

This is apparent in education at school, in companies and even in newspapers, television and other forms of mass media. It is their very basic attitude to portray religion as if there is something wrong with the whole idea. Yet, in reality, the value system that they adhere to is wrong. They should stop analyzing everything from a small perspective, much like an ant walking around on the ground trying to observe the world. If they know the much grander perspective of the world and the universe, they would not make such mistakes. Only religion can teach us that, and only Happy Science can present such a large perspective on the world.

Success as a Part of the Tree of Life

Once you start living with the true outlook of the world from the perspective of the universe, you will probably have conflicts with the values of this world in many occasions. In the economy and in the government, within law or education, in family problems or in your views on marriage, your values will clash in many places with the ones of this world. However, I would like to convey one thing to you in the midst of it all. As a religious leader, in order to open the doors for everybody's happiness in the future, I am looking out from the era now, forward into the 22nd, 23rd, 25th, 30th, 40th, 50th century and much beyond. Thinking about an era very far ahead, I feel that a solid foundation of the superiority of faith is necessary. Even if we are successful in this world, we only live for a few decades and rarely more than 100 years. If that success goes against the great laws of the universe, and it is undesirable for the success of a branch from the Tree of Life, then it will become a broken branch or withered leaves before long. Success that goes against the cosmic laws of life will dissolve to bitter emptiness. That is why the foundation of faith is the most important.

Seek Success with the Superiority of Faith

You can become experts and make excellent achievements or acquire an abundance of knowledge. Yet, if it does not correspond to the fundamental faith, unfortunately, you will not be able to achieve happiness in the future.

For example, consider a person who became extremely famous in this world as an author of murder mysteries. Suppose that the author's novels became a television show series, got great ratings, and the novels were long-time best sellers. That person may be highly regarded in this world, but spiritually, the author is likely to suffer in Hell after he or she dies. That author may suffer in a world much like the one the author had created in the novels. That author had such an extreme interest in murder cases that the author investigated and thought only about how to kill people, or how to deceive people into a deathly trap. The soul of a person that only thinks about those things inevitably heads to Hell. Therefore, no matter how highly esteemed people may be in this world, sadly, they cannot return to the heavenly realms.

In this way, success in this world is different from success in the next world. You must firmly keep a superiority of faith and have an unfaltering pillar of true faith within you. Success must be found with true faith. If you only think about your success or failure in this world without having true faith, you will never be able to gain true success.

Worldly Values and Faith

It is the same with your academic background. People who receive good grades in school, attend the best prep schools, and attend famous universities, are considered by many people as winners in this world. Perhaps there are people who were valedictorians of prestigious universities and find employment with top-notch companies or join government offices. They may be considered very important and thought of as the most prominent people in society. However, if you look at these people from a spiritual perspective, there are actually many aspects that are not so "great." It would be a different story for people who had learned religious values outside of school, and had worked hard to polish their outlooks on life while having feelings of love for others. Yet, many people who have grown up with only the education of this world will sadly end up in the realms of Hell, even if they are considered to be geniuses that can represent the whole country. Please do not be deluded by the value system of this world that judges people solely based on the company names, or the superiority of skills. There are various kinds of success based on materialistic values in this world. This includes the success in the business world seen in the level of prestige of your company, success in academics seen in your educational background, or the acquirement of high social status by perhaps becoming successful physicians.

However, I would like you to stop at all different aspects and check to see whether you have a superiority of faith, and think whether you are considering everything with faith as your priority. If you are not thinking from the perspective of putting faith first, you become a branch or leaf in the Tree of Life that only thinks about yourself. This results in a separation from the big Tree of Life, which leads to the withering of your part of the tree. When this happens, you stand a high possibility of falling into the realms of Hell. So please re-think once more about the superiority of your faith against all values of this world.

5. The Law of Compensation

Compensation for Faith is the Greatest Blessing

Prioritizing faith also means to abandon something for faith.

In the first chapter, "What to Remember in Life," of the book, *The Laws of Life*, I wrote about the Law of Compensation. This law says that if you want to gain something, you need to abandon something. It also says that there is nothing to gain without perseverance and devotion, and that the compensation of what you pay for is equivalent to the value of what you will gain. In the end, the best compensations are the compensations to what you paid for faith. Giving up something for faith means that you will gain the greatest blessings in the next world.

What compensations have you paid to put your faith into practice? What have you done in this lifetime in order to put faith above all? What have you done to believe in and act on the conviction that faith surpasses all, and that faith is the most important and the most valuable? A future that corresponds to your compensations will certainly come. It will add up perfectly, and there are no exceptions to this.

This Law of Compensation works in the matters of this world too. This world uses it as the principles of choice, which states that if you want to gain something, you must give something up. It is also used in the principles of economy or success, which states that you will succeed if you concentrate on one thing. However, the most important thing is, after all, what you pay in compensation for the sake of your faith. You may sometimes have to make effort, devote yourself, and give something up for faith. There will be times when you have to give up things that you would have chased after if you lived solely for the desires of this world. There may be times when you must abandon something for faith.

The Paradox of Living as an Elite Soul

However, please do not lament over this. Although this perspective is the complete opposite of the one of this world, please accept the paradox that you are now, polishing your soul and about to enter the path of success as a soul. Suffering through many hardships and ordeals in this world actually means that your soul has been trained rigorously. This indicates that these people are actually extraordinary elites and are chosen souls. "Elites" who cruise through life with everything going well and effortlessly gain acknowledgement are not true elites. There are people who overcome various trials of life, persecutions, illnesses, financial struggles or other hardships, and they grasp true faith through these experiences. The people who made effort to help and save many others are the ones who Buddha and God have chosen, and are the elite souls. Therefore, I would like you to have a view of the elite that is different from the values of this world.

Live with a Spiritual Perspective

You must firmly hold the superiority of faith in your

heart. In the Laws of Compensation, the important point is *how much you can cast away worldly things and live a life of Truth.*

Shakyamuni Buddha and Jesus Christ preached this as well. They both taught to cast away the things of this world. This is the Law of Compensation. Those who have an attachment to the things of this world sink by the "weight" of their attachment. However, those who are not attached to worldly things and live a life viewing the world with spiritual eyes, heavenly eyes, from the eyes of the other world, and the eyes of Buddha and God, will without doubt, be able to sit close to Buddha and God. This is the most important point of the Law of Compensation. Please remember this.

I have talked about various topics under the theme of living a life of Truth. I would like for you to have a perspective that your life is connected to the great Cosmic Tree and to the lives of many people with strong spiritual ties. I hope with all my heart that you will shine brightly as a part of the Cosmic Tree and have great courage to live a life of faith.

Afterword

Saburo Yoshikawa, my father and honorary consultant to Happy Science, passed away on August 12, 2003, just a few days before turning 82 years old.

My father entrusted two bequests in me, as his son.

His first will was to build a school, and plan building schools up to college.

I am currently in the process of founding the Happy Science Junior High and Senior High School, which are scheduled to open in the spring of 2010. I am also planning to build the Happy Science University three years following that.

The second will my father entrusted in me with was to publish *The Laws of Courage*.

It has been almost six years now since I heard my father say his last words. Finally, *The Laws of Courage* has been completed and made ready for publishing. I am overwhelmed with happiness. I dedicate this book to my father, who sits high in Heaven, smiling down upon us.

Father, I am sorry this took so long. I am 52 years old now. I have laid down my life for my mission. Having preached the Laws of Courage, I will not have any regrets even if I were to die today.

With gratitude,

Ryuho Okawa
Happy Science
December 2008

Happy Science

INTERNATIONAL HEADQUARTERS:

Tokyo
1-6-7 Togoshi,
Shinagawa, Tokyo 142-0041, Japan
Tel: 81-3-6384-5770
Fax: 81-3-6384-5776
Email: tokyo@happy-science.org
www.kofuku-no-kagaku.or.jp/en

NORTH AMERICA:

New York
79 Franklin Street,
New York, NY 10013, U.S.A.
Tel: 1-212-343-7972
Fax: 1-212-343-7973
Email: ny@happy-science.org
www.happyscience-ny.org

Los Angeles
1590 E. Del Mar Blvd.,
Pasadena, CA 91106, U.S.A.
Tel: 1-626-395-7775
Fax: 1-626-395-7776
Email: la@happy-science.org
www.happyscience-la.org

South Bay
2340 Sepulveda Blvd., #B,
Torrance, CA 90501 U.S.A.
Tel: 1-310-539-7771
Fax: 1-310-539-7772
Email: la@happy-science.org

San Francisco
525 Clinton St.,
Redwood City, CA 94062, U.S.A.
Tel / Fax: 1-650-363-2777
Email: sf@happy-science.org
www.happyscience-sf.org

Hawaii
1221 Kapiolani Blvd., Suite 920
Honolulu, HI 96814, U.S.A.
Tel: 1-808-591-9772
Fax: 1-808-591-9776
Email: hi@happy-science.org
www.happyscience-hi.org

Florida
Email: florida@happy-science.org

Albuquerque
Email: abq@happy-science.org

Boston
Email: boston@happy-science.org

Chicago
Email: chicago@happy-science.org

Atlanta
Email: atlanta@happy-science.org

Toronto
2420 A Bloor Street,
W. Toronto ON, M6S 1P9, Canada
Tel: 1-416-551-7467
Fax: 1-905-257-2006
Email: toronto@happy-science.org

Vancouver
Email: vancouver@happy-science.org

Mexico
Email: mexico@happy-science.org

EUROPE:

London
3 Margaret Street,
London, W1W 8RE,
United Kingdom
Tel: 44-20-7323-9255
Fax: 44-20-7323-9344
Email: eu@happy-science.org
www.happyscience-eu.org

France
Email: france@happy-science.org

Germany
Email:
germany@happy-science.org

Austria
Email:
austria-vienna@happy-science.org

Zurich
Email:
switzerland@happy-science.org

AFRICA:

Uganda
Email: uganda@happy-science.org

SOUTH AMERICA:

Sao Paulo West
Rua Gandavo, 363 Vila Mariana
Sao Paulo, CEP 04023-001, Brazil
Tel: 55-11-5574-0054
Fax: 55-11-5574-8164
Email: sp@happy-science.org

Sao Paulo East
Rua Fernao Tavares
124 Tatuape 03306-030
Sao Paulo, Brazil
Tel: 55-11-2295-8500
Fax: 55-11-2295-8505
Email: sp@happy-science.org/
cienciaf@uol.com.br

Sorocaba
Tel/Fax: 55-11-5072-3292

OCEANIA:

Sydney
Suite 17, 71-77 Penshurst Street
Willoughby, NSW 2068, Australia
Tel: 61-2-9967-0766
Fax: 61-2-9967-0866
Email: sydney@happy-science.org
www.happyscience.org.au

Melbourne
Tel: 61-4-3484-1896
Email: mel@happy-science.org

ASIA:

Seoul
162-17 Sadang3-dong,
Dongjak-gu, Seoul, Korea
Tel: 82-2-3478-8777
Fax: 82-2-3478-9777
Email: korea@happy-science.org

Daegu
878-20 2F, Manchon 3 Dong
Susong-ku, Daegu
Kwangyok-Si, Korea
Tel: 82-53-291-3688
Email: daegu@happy-science.org

Taipei
No.89, Lane 155, Dunhua N. Rd.,
Songshan District, Taipei City 105,
Taiwan
Tel: 886-2-2719-9377
Fax: 886-2-2719-5570
Email: taiwan@happy-science.org
www.happyscience-taiwan.org

Hong Kong
Email:
hongkong@happy-science.org

Delhi
Email: newdelhi@happy-science.org
www.happyscience-india.org

BOOKS BY RYUHO OKAWA

The Laws of the Sun
The Spiritual Laws & History Governing Past, Present & Future
ISBN:1-930051-62-X Lantern Books, 2001

The Golden Laws
History through the Eyes of the Eternal Buddha
ISBN:1-930051-61-1 Lantern Books, 2002

The Laws of Eternity
Unfolding the Secrets of the Multidimensional Universe
ISBN:1-930051-63-8 Lantern Books, 2001

Ten Principles of Universal Wisdom
The Truth of Happiness, Enlightenment, and the Creation of an Ideal World
ISBN:1-59056-094-9 Lantern Books, 2005

The Starting Point of Happiness
A Practical and Intuitive Guide to Discovering Love, Wisdom, and Faith
ISBN:1-930051-18-2 Lantern Books, 2001

Guideposts to Happiness
Prescriptions for a Wonderful Life
ISBN:1-59056-056-6 Lantern Books, 2004

Love, Nurture, and Forgive
A Handbook to Add a New Richness to Your Life
ISBN:1-930051-78-6 Lantern Books, 2002

The Origin of Love
On the Beauty of Compassion
ISBN:1-59056-052-3 Lantern Books, 2003

An Unshakable Mind
How to Overcome Life's Difficulties
ISBN:1-930051-77-8 Lantern Books, 2003

Invincible Thinking
There Is No Such Thing As Defeat
ISBN:1-59056-051-5 Lantern Books, 2003

The Laws of Happiness
The Four Principles for a Successful Life
ISBN:1-59056-073-6 Lantern Books, 2004

Tips to Find Happiness
Creating a Harmonious Home for Your Spouse, Your Children, and Yourself
ISBN:1-59056-080-9 Lantern Books, 2004

The Philosophy of Progress
Higher Thinking for Developing Infinite Prosperity
ISBN:1-59056-057-4 Lantern Books, 2005

The Essence of Buddha
The Path to Enlightenment
ISBN:0-7515-3355-6 Time Warner Books, 2003

The Challenge of the Mind
A Practical Approach to the Essential Buddhist Teaching of Karma
ISBN:0-7515-3573-7 Time Warner Books, 2005

The Challenge of Enlightenment
Realize Your Inner Potential
ISBN:0-316-73149-8 Little, Brown Book Group, 2007

"I'm Fine" Spirit
How to Get Through Tough Times
Happy Science, 2008

A Ray of Light
Happy Science, 2008

Healing Yourself
The True Relationship Between Mind and Body
Happy Science, 2008

My Lover, Cross the Valley of Tears
Happy Science, 2008